MW01062275

"The study of astrology can be a great tool for anyone em-barking on a quest for personal insight and confidence, but it's especially useful for teenagers, who often find themselves struggling with their identities and wondering which direction life will take them. In fact, I wish I would've had a guide like this when I began studying astrology as a teen!"

—KELLI FOX, CREATOR OF WWW.ASTROLOGY.COM

"*Lucky Stars* is a great introductory book on real astrology for young people. Solid, useable tips are outlined for each Sun sign that can help you answer questions such as 'Why do I always do that?,' 'How can I stop doing it?,' and 'How can I get a real, live love life?' This book hands you keys to indi-vidual life lessons and empowers you with the knowledge that ultimately, you make your own luck."

—TAMLYN JORDAN, "ZENITA," TEEN ADVICE COLUMNIST FOR ASTRONET.COM

"Amanda Owen offers straight talk about getting to know yourself through the stars. This book will help you under-stand yourself better, which is the key to having better friendships, relationships, and life goals. If you want to know what is unique about you and what will make you happy and strong, then pick up this book."

—ELIZABETH LESSER, COFOUNDER OF THE OMEGA INSTITUTE AND AUTHOR OF *THE NEW AMERICAN SPIRITUALITY*

"Amanda Owen has written a lively, entertaining, and practical introduction to astrology for young people. *Lucky Stars* is destined to enlighten teens and young adults of the twenty-first century about the connection between the twelve signs of the zodiac and their own lives."

—DONNA CUNNINGHAM, M.S.W, AUTHOR OF
MOON SIGNS AND COLUMNIST FOR
DELL HOROSCOPE MAGAZINE

"*Lucky Stars* is a surefire book charm for young people as well as anyone who thinks young."

—RONNIE GALE DREYER, AUTHOR OF
HEALING SIGNS AND *VEDIC ASTROLOGY*

"Kids of planet Earth, I hope you're ready. Prepare for your cosmic education."

—MICHAEL LUTIN, COLUMNIST FOR *VANITY FAIR*
AND *AMERICAN WAY* MAGAZINES AND AUTHOR OF
MADE IN HEAVEN AND *CHILDHOOD RISING*

Lucky Stars

Use Astrology to Get the Scoop on Life, Love, and Friendship

Amanda Owen

THREE RIVERS PRESS • NEW YORK

Published by Three Rivers Press, New York, New York.
Member of the Crown Publishing Group.

Random House, Inc. New York, Toronto, London, Sydney, Auckland
www.randomhouse.com

THREE RIVERS PRESS is a registered trademark and the Three Rivers Press colophon is a trademark of Random House, Inc.

Printed in the United States of America

Design by Lindregn/Fuller Design

Library of Congress Cataloging-in-Publication Data
Owen, Amanda.
    Lucky stars : use astrology to get the scoop on life, love, and
    friendship / by Amanda Owen.
        p. cm.
    1. Astrology. 2. Horoscopes. 3. Zodiac. I. Title.
    BF1708.1.098 2001   2001023462
    133.5'2—dc21

ISBN 0-609-80687-4

10 9 8 7 6 5 4 3 2

This book is dedicated to
my mother, Virginia,
and
my father, John

Here comes the Sun...

THE BEATLES

Acknowledgments

There are many who helped me in the course of writing *Lucky Stars*. I would not feel this book to be complete without thanking them. I am indebted to my agent, Henry Dunow, who helped shepherd me through everything. I am grateful to the following teens for sharing their lives, thoughts, and suggestions: Leila Burke, Jennie Johnson, Julia Kartman, Stefanie Santaniello, and Matt Smith. For their belief in and enthusiasm for this project and particularly for their editorial help and assistance, I thank Karyn Hill, Jill Cherpack, and my editor at Three Rivers Press, Sarah Silbert. For their support throughout the writing of this book, I am especially grateful to Stephen Russo, Meridee Winters, Gabriela Biber, Elizabeth Rose Campbell, Sandra Belsky, Willie Nile, Judy Slagle, Peter Cherpack, and my students and clients. And finally, I thank massage therapist Carlton Ann Daily, who kept my back in shape through the long hours of sitting at the computer.

Contents

Introduction

Dear Reader,

How many times have you read your horoscope and wondered, "How can somebody know me just by knowing my Sun sign?" The fact is, an astrologer *does* know something about you just by knowing your Sun sign. The Sun sign describes an important and central theme of your life. The Sun is our solar system's star, and your Sun sign is your own personal "star." A Sun sign's characteristics don't tell the whole story about a person—only part of the story. That's why, when you read a horoscope based only on the Sun sign, sometimes the information will be correct and other times it won't even come close. When astrologers provide complete consultations for their clients, they look at much more than the Sun sign. The date, time, and place of birth are used to calculate an astrology birth chart, which depicts the positions of all of the planets in addition to those of the Sun and Moon. Astrologers examine the locations of the planets with respect to the signs they occupy; they observe the planets' angular relationships to each other and their relationship to the earth. It's complicated and takes years to learn.

Although astrology has been around a long time (historians trace it back to at least 2500 B.C.), it has been adapted over the years to meet the changing needs of humanity. It has survived the rise and fall of civilizations: from times when astrology's benefits were available to everyone to periods when it was reserved for royalty and the wealthy. In modern times it is used by people from all walks of life.

You are coming of age in the dawn of a new century. Collectively, you are more mature and sophisticated than many young people of previous generations. You are uniquely suited to make the most of what astrology has to offer. The information in this book will help you take advantage of opportunities and answer some of your questions such as:

> Why do some things come easily to me, while I struggle in other areas?
> I have a crush on someone—but is he or she a good match for me?
> How do I know what career will be the right one?
> How can I have more friends?
> How can I be more confident?
> How can I get to know the important people in my life better?

Astrology addresses every part of your life, from your deepest dreams and desires to your spirituality, from your friendships to your love life. *Lucky Stars* provides insight into all of these important areas. A compatibility guide is included in each chapter to give you extra information about your relationships with every sign. Use this guide for your romantic relationships and to learn more about those close to you, including friends and family members. Each chapter ends with ten special tips summarizing the most important messages that were discussed.

We all have a "lucky star." Your Sun sign is your own personal lucky star. Although *luck* can be defined as something that happens by chance, I prefer the old saying, "Luck is when preparation meets opportunity." There is little that prepares you more for life's opportunities than knowing yourself. I hope this book helps you to create your own luck by using your star as a guide.

Amanda

SUN SIGNS

♈	**Aries**	March 20 to April 20
♉	**Taurus**	April 20 to May 21
♊	**Gemini**	May 21 to June 21
♋	**Cancer**	June 21 to July 23
♌	**Leo**	July 23 to August 23
♍	**Virgo**	August 23 to September 23
♎	**Libra**	September 23 to October 23
♏	**Scorpio**	October 23 to November 22
♐	**Sagittarius**	November 22 to December 21
♑	**Capricorn**	December 21 to January 20
♒	**Aquarius**	January 20 to February 19
♓	**Pisces**	February 19 to March 20

---

* There are 365¼ days in an average year, with a leap year every fourth year. As a result, the Sun enters a new sign a day earlier or later depending on the year. For example, in some years the Sun enters Aries on March 20, while in other years the Sun enters on March 21. If you were born on a day the Sun changed signs, to identify your Sun sign you need to have the Sun's position calculated for your time, day, and year of birth. Look in the resources section to find out how.

What's Your Sign?

When people ask, "What's your sign?" they are asking what zodiac sign the Sun was in on the day you were born. Although the earth revolves around the Sun, from our perspective it appears that the Sun circles the earth. As the Sun makes this apparent journey around the earth, it travels across the backdrop of the twelve signs of the zodiac. The term zodiac comes from the Greek *zodiacos,* which means "circle of animals." Most of the zodiac signs have animal symbols.

The Sun enters Aries, the first zodiac sign, on March 20 or March 21 (see footnote on page xv) of each year, which signals the first day of spring in the northern hemisphere. (In the southern hemisphere this marks the first day of autumn.) It travels through Aries for approximately thirty days until it enters the next sign, Taurus, on April 19 or 20. Anyone born between those dates has an Aries Sun sign—just as someone who is born when the Sun travels though Taurus between approximately April 20 and May 21 has the Sun sign Taurus. When we celebrate our birthdays, we are commemorating the day the Sun arrives at the same part of the zodiac it occupied on the day of our birth.

The table on page xv provides dates for each Sun sign. If your birthday is on the day the Sun changes signs (which is called being born on the cusp) you will need to find out the time of your birth to identify your Sun sign. Look in the resources section at the end of this book to find out how.

Just as the Sun is at the center of our solar system, in astrology the Sun represents your "center." It describes how you express yourself and how you think about yourself. Every Sun sign has its own unique and distinctive characteristics. One sign is not better or worse than another, but each has both positive and negative qualities. Expressing the positive qualities of your sign leads to self-confidence. Acting out the negative traits of your sign makes you feel worse about yourself. Astrology gives specific information tailored to your Sun sign that tells you which traits to emphasize and minimize to create a successful life.

Chances are, as you read this book you will identify with some of the descriptions that are not used for your own Sun sign. No one has only his or her Sun sign's characteristics. When you were born, the Moon occupied a zodiac sign that is different from your Sun sign. (Only people born at the new Moon have the same Moon sign and Sun sign.) Mercury, Venus, Mars, Jupiter, Saturn, Uranus, Neptune, and Pluto were also in their own sign. The planets and Moon represent different parts of your personality. In astrology, the combination of the planet, Sun, and Moon sign placements illustrates the full complexity of a person.

For example, your Sun may be in the independent, free-spirited sign of Aquarius, while your Moon occupies the cautious and security-focused sign of Taurus. Reading about the differences between these two signs can help you understand how you have different needs that must be fulfilled. In this example, to make life easier you would need to balance your desire for independence with your need for security and stability.

In addition to the signs of your Sun, Moon, and planets, you also have a "rising sign," which is determined by the time of your birth. The rising sign (also called the ascendant) describes how you approach life and the type of first impression you give people.

Your astrological birth chart is a picture of the sky at the time of your birth as viewed from Earth. Featured in it are your Sun, Moon, planets, and rising sign. If you have a copy of your birth chart and know your rising sign, Moon sign, and the signs of the planets, reading those signs' chapters will give you information that you will be able to use right away. If you don't have a copy of your birth chart, the resources section at the end of this book tells you how to get one.

Interacting with the World: Elements and Modes

Do you ever wonder why some people are easy to talk to, while others don't even seem to speak the same language? For example, it's interesting to observe a conversation between someone who is very emotional and another who is extremely logical. Each experiences the world so differently that communication can be difficult. Some people love the same activities that you do, while others are mystified by your choices. Some would like nothing better than to spend their summer exploring a foreign country, while others just want to get a summer job and save money. We all respond to life in our own way. These variations in personality are shown by the elements and modes.

SIGN	ELEMENT	MODE
Aries	Fire	Cardinal
Taurus	Earth	Fixed
Gemini	Air	Mutable
Cancer	Water	Cardinal
Leo	Fire	Fixed
Virgo	Earth	Mutable
Libra	Air	Cardinal
Scorpio	Water	Fixed
Sagittarius	Fire	Mutable
Capricorn	Earth	Cardinal
Aquarius	Air	Fixed
Pisces	Water	Mutable

Your Sun sign belongs to one of four elements (fire, earth, air, water) and to one of three modes (cardinal, fixed, mutable). Your Sun sign's element describes how you respond to the world. The mode shows how you approach the world. The element and mode together produce the characteristics of each Sun sign.

Sun signs that share the same element are compatible because they respond to the world similarly. They instinctively understand one another. Fire and air signs are compatible because they both tend to be sociable, outgoing, and active. Earth and water signs are compatible because both are more likely to be reserved, security-focused, and self-protective.

Sun signs that occupy the same mode may get along or clash. Although they share some personality characteristics and approaches to life, they can work at cross-purposes and get on each other's nerves.

The following descriptions explain the features of each element and mode.

THE ELEMENTS

Fire: Aries, Leo, and Sagittarius

If you are a fire sign, you respond to the world through your idealism. You are strong-willed, enthusiastic, and like to be active. At your best, you have enormous faith in yourself; you inspire people, are optimistic, and blaze new trails. At your worst, you are overly self-focused, reckless, and impatient with others.

Earth: Taurus, Virgo, and Capricorn

If you are an earth sign, you respond to the world through your five senses: what you see, hear, taste, touch, and smell. You are practical, dependable, and focused on security. At your best, you are patient, disciplined, and have a great sense about how the world works. At your worst, you value material security over everything else, are suspicious of what you have not personally experienced, and are reluctant to make changes.

Air: Gemini, Libra, and Aquarius

If you are an air sign, you respond to the world through your mind. You like to socialize; you are interested in the world of concepts and ideas and are motivated to communicate them to others. At your best, you are a natural teacher and an innovative thinker. At your worst, living too much in the world of the mind, you are opinionated, impersonal, and impractical.

Water: Cancer, Scorpio, and Pisces

If you are a water sign, you respond to the world through your feelings. You are sensitive, caring, and imaginative. At your best, you have great gut instincts and are compassionate and amazingly intuitive. At your worst, you are hypersensitive, emotionally reactive, and let your worries prevent you from accomplishing your goals.

THE MODES

Cardinal: Aries, Cancer, Libra, and Capricorn

Cardinal signs approach life with a great deal of drive. If you are cardinal, you are energetic and love to be on the go and initiate new activities. At your best, you are enterprising and accomplish your goals. At your worst, you are pushy and don't know how to hang back.

Fixed: Taurus, Leo, Scorpio, and Aquarius

Fixed signs approach life with determination. If you are fixed, you have great endurance and strength; you have the talent for sticking with what you started. At your best, you are loyal, dependable, and have remarkable self-control. At your worst, you are stubborn, rigid in your opinions, and reluctant to make changes.

Mutable: Gemini, Virgo, Sagittarius, and Pisces

Mutable signs approach life by adapting to circumstances. If you are mutable, you are open to change and are flexible, friendly, and easygoing. At your best, you get along with others and have an accommodating nature. At your worst, you are overly impressionable and unable to stand your ground.

Lucky Stars

Aries

The Pioneer

March 20 to April 20

Symbol: The Ram
Ruling planet: Mars
Element: Fire—*outgoing, enthusiastic, strong*
Mode: Cardinal—*energetic, initiating, active*
Birthstone: Diamond
Color: Red

FAMOUS ARIES PEOPLE:

March 20	Henrik Ibsen	March 28	Reba McEntire
March 21	Rosie O'Donnell	March 29	Lucy Lawless
March 22	Reese Witherspoon	March 30	Tracy Chapman
March 23	Chaka Khan	March 31	César Chávez
March 24	Tommy Hilfiger	April 1	Clara Hale
March 25	Aretha Franklin	April 2	Dana Carvey
March 26	Steven Tyler	April 3	Marlon Brando
March 27	Mariah Carey	April 4	Maya Angelou

April 5	Booker T. Washington	April 13	Thomas Jefferson
April 6	Ram Das	April 14	Sarah Michelle Gellar
April 7	Jackie Chan	April 15	Leonardo da Vinci
April 8	Robin Wright Penn	April 16	Martin Lawrence
April 9	Paul Robeson	April 17	Isak Dinesen
April 10	Mandy Moore	April 18	Conan O'Brien
April 11	Alex Haley	April 19	Ashley Judd
April 12	Claire Danes	April 20	Peter Frampton

THESE BEHAVIORS AND ATTITUDES INCREASE CONFIDENCE

Adventurousness
Courageousness
Risk-taking
Assertiveness
Spontaneity
Idealism
Independence

THESE BEHAVIORS AND ATTITUDES DECREASE CONFIDENCE

Impatience
Selfishness
Pushiness
Childishness
Impracticality
Inconsiderateness
Uncooperativeness

THE PIONEER

Like Aries Jane Goodall, whose groundbreaking work with chimpanzees captured the world's attention; Gloria Steinem, who played an important role in the movement for women's equality; and, Quentin Tarantino, who introduced a new and innovative style of filmmaking—you, too, are a pioneer. You venture into areas where less-brave souls would dare not go. No challenge is too great for you. You are ready to try almost anything. Life is an adventure, and you want to live it to the fullest.

The fact that something has never been done before does not deter you in the least. This first sign of the zodiac is the sign of new beginnings: the first day of spring, the birth of new animals, or the fresh growth of flowers and leaves. Your love of starting something new and your enterprising personality lead you to paths and life journeys that are fun and exciting.

As an Aries, you are confident and optimistic about what you can accomplish. Although you can overestimate your abilities at times, if you run into an obstacle, you have the great knack for dusting yourself off and leaping headfirst into your next project. You do not dwell on the past, but are very future-oriented and interested in what is just ahead.

Aries people lead, motivate, and inspire like nobody else. Others become excited by your vision and readily sign up for the adventure. You help others to feel confident about themselves and their ideas. "You can do it!" are words you often say to yourself and to others. You lead the way.

You have a "can-do" attitude. The word *failure* is not in your vocabulary. If something does not go as you had planned (what little planning there was), you are genuinely surprised. You are so resilient, though, that you pick yourself up and try again. You are willing to attempt things more than once to become successful. In fact, you love the challenge.

Because the focus of an Aries is on beginning something new, you often do not consider fully what you are getting into nor perceive the full scope of what you are taking on, which can be a good thing. Sometimes people who think too much and obsess about the details never leave the starting gate and never get their ideas off the ground because they become overwhelmed. You act first and then take care of whatever comes up.

Others feel protective of you and may wish you were a bit more cautious. Although caution is not an Aries trait, that doesn't mean you shouldn't use your head—and not as a battering ram to push something through! It is important to use your mind, to think things out, to cultivate the strategy and planning that exists in every Aries. Your mind is the perfect complement to your can-do attitude.

Let's Do It NOW!

As a rule, Aries do not like to follow rules. You are enthusiastic, eager, and ready to act quickly. Usually you do not follow directions because you have not *read or listened to* them, which often means that you have to go back to the beginning and start all over again.

This characteristic impatience can make it hard for you to wait your turn. Standing in a line at the movies or in the cafeteria can be a frustrating experience. When Aries people are raring to go, they tend to hurry others—which can make people move slower, not faster.

Impatience can also make it hard for you to stay focused on long-term goals. Your natural enthusiasm and self-starter qualities can help. Use these abilities to break down a long-term goal into sections or mini-goals to help to keep your passion alive.

For example, if you plan to compete in a race four months from now, you may lose interest during training. But if you run each day with the mini-goal of improving your speed or distance, it will be easy for you to retain your enthusiasm, which will help you to succeed when the day of the race arrives. Use your creative mind to invent new and better ways to keep focused on a long-term goal.

Leadership

Aries is one of the signs of leadership. The ability to step forward and to take advantage of opportunities helps you move toward your future. Getting ahead is important to you. You have a competitive instinct, which is one of your greatest strengths—you strive to do even better today than you did yesterday. "How can I improve and be more successful?" you ask yourself. Your competitive spirit will take you on some amazing journeys during your life. Aries Sandra Day O'Connor took advantage of opportunities to become the first woman Supreme Court justice. General Colin Powell's competitive spirit carried him all the way to the highest U.S. military office when he became the chairman of the Joint Chiefs of Staff. Later, President George W. Bush asked him to serve as secretary of state under his administration.

What opportunities can you take advantage of now to improve your circumstances? Use your competitive instinct to go for your personal best, and you will create a fun and interesting life.

Looking Out for Number One

Traditionally in astrology, Aries are told that they have a hard time considering anybody's needs but their own. But this is not necessarily true anymore. In this age of teamwork and global consciousness, Aries can use their creative, pioneering, brave energy to become champions not only for themselves, but also for others. Fulfilling your own desires does not have to be at odds with the people around you. Would Jane Goodall have studied and helped chimpanzees if she thought only of herself? Gloria Steinem wanted a better life, and by helping all women she helped herself. Rosie O'Donnell uses her celebrity to support a variety of charities.

Some of you Aries will pioneer into the frontier of outer space; some will lead the world in developing new forms of technology; some will initiate new approaches to education;

some will create new genres of music; some will open up new ways for people to understand each other and get along. Like Aries William Shatner's character in *Star Trek,* your mission is to bravely go where no one has gone before.

Your Soul Mission: Taking Advantage of Your Warrior Spirit

In Roman mythology, Mars, the ruling planet of Aries, is the name for the god of war. The Greek goddess Athena, who supervised and directed battle strategy, is also linked to Aries. Like this god and goddess, you are gifted with bravery, daring, and boldness. You have a warrior spirit and are always ready to fight for a cause, for the underdog, and for yourself.

But any feisty god or goddess gets upset sometimes. The immortals of mythology often used their anger to wreak havoc on some poor mortal. Though their rampages may have been momentarily satisfying, there were often disastrous consequences. There are better ways to express anger than through temper tantrums. Anger, when used as a motivator, taps into the most creative and inspired parts of who you are. When you channel this powerful energy to defend yourself and others, you can move mountains. Many an Aries has shaken a fist skyward and cried, "I am not going to let [fill in the blank] hold me back!"

Fighting for a cause is giving a gift of yourself to the world, to humankind. Allow the things in this world that you do not think are right to inspire you to employ your exceptional drive and energy. Aries journalist Bob Woodward was motivated to expose the Watergate scandal. His work helped force President Nixon to resign.

If you are feeling angry, even if you do not know why, run around the block, beat up your pillow, become a member of a hockey team, play a pickup game of basketball, join a band, or play video games. Don't take your anger out on someone else like the gods of mythology did.

If you do know what you are angry about, don't bury it. Talk to someone—a trusted friend, relative, parent, or counselor. Do what you can to change or affect the circumstances that are bothering you. Part of being an Aries is learning how to work with anger, so it is important to address it, not stuff it!

FRIENDSHIP

An Aries is a fun and exciting friend, always ready at a moment's notice to try something new. You gravitate toward the "leader of the pack" position. You inspire your friends and help them stand up for themselves and to be confident. If friends are upset about something, you encourage them to get up, go out, and not let anyone or anything hold them back or get them down. You introduce your friends to new and exciting experiences. You encourage them to be active. You love to be on the move, whether you are skateboarding, hiking, or biking, and are naturally attracted to friends who are also active.

Because an Aries gravitates toward excitement rather than stability, you may bail out on plans with a friend if something else comes up that you would prefer to do. This can stress your friendship bonds. Think of your friends' needs as well as your own, and you will always have more friends than you can count.

Check out the compatibility guide later in this chapter to see how your friends' Sun signs match up with yours.

HOME LIFE

You may be a handful for your parents. You have a strong personality along with inner strength, which can bring about some arguments and clashes with family members. Ideally, you need the chance to express your independence within your family home life. To gain the opportunity to spread your wings, prove to your parents or guardian that you can use good judgment and are responsible. Actions speak louder than words—and because you are naturally active, this should not be difficult for you.

Energetic and on the go, you may be hard to find at home. Or, you may have a family that thrives on being busy with a number of activities. Wherever your lively nature originates, sitting around is definitely not your style!

The objects of your many activities and half-finished projects are likely to fill your bedroom. Keeping everything in order is not your forte. Bright strong colors attract you, so your posters or pictures are likely to be attention-grabbing rather than images of soothing and restful scenes. Basically, your bedroom is probably a place where you change your clothes rather than spend time.

CAREER

Sitting behind a desk eight hours a day is not for you. A job or career that allows freedom of movement and independence is preferable, whether working on cars, running a martial-arts studio, or hosting your own television show like Aries Conan O' Brien and David Letterman.

You are a creative idea person, so any career in public relations, marketing, or selling is a good choice. Tommy Hilfiger, famous for the clothing that shares his name, is a great example of an Aries who knows how to successfully market a product.

Because you know how to inspire people, any cause or idea about which you feel strongly benefits by your natural talents. Aries César Chávez inspired countless people when he created and led a successful farm workers' union that made life better for thousands of people. Aries Thomas Jefferson continues to inspire people everywhere with his words in the Declaration of Independence.

It is important for you to pursue a career that sparks your enthusiasm. You need to feel passionate about whatever you are doing. The following Aries natives embody the passion, creativity, and inventiveness of your sign: Leonardo da Vinci, the original Renaissance man, explored numerous interests from painting and sculpture to engineering and science. Booker T. Washington founded the Tuskegee Institute, a pioneering industrial and agricultural school for African-American students in 1881. Clara Hale founded Hale House, a place to nurture and care for babies born to drug-addicted women infected with the AIDS virus, during a time when people were afraid to have contact with those who had AIDS. All of these Aries pioneers followed their passion and spent their lives doing what they most loved.

Think of careers that spark your passion. Your intuition will show you which ones to explore.

RELATIONSHIPS

Aries: The Adventure of Love

Daring, courageous, and spontaneous, you are not the type to wait around for subtle clues that someone is interested in you. You will court, campaign, and try to win over the person you are attracted to. You are certainly noticeable. Like a fairy-tale maiden or a knight in shining armor galloping in on a horse, your whole being says, "I will go to the ends of the earth and back for my love." People are attracted to your spirited energy.

Maintaining your independence is important to you. You need to feel that you are your own person and that your boyfriend or girlfriend appreciates and supports this quality in you.

Sometimes impulsive in matters of the heart, you may positively swoon over somebody today and then get bored and turn your attention to someone else tomorrow. You find excitement in the beginning of a relationship, since you love everything new. If your sweetie wants to talk about a relationship problem, you may interpret this as interfering with your independence. Because relationships are, in part, about cooperation and tuning into your partner's needs, desires, and dreams, apply your adventurous spirit to your relationship. Get excited about discovering all there is to know about the person you care for.

For you, Aries, it is particularly important to develop strength, confidence, and self-esteem in your relationships. If you do not express these strengths, you may become attracted to people who insist on making all of the decisions and always having things their own way. This kind of relationship will squash your pioneering spirit and natural sense of independence. For you, having a successful relationship is a matter of balancing your need for independence while being sensitive to your partner's needs.

Sign Compatibility

There are some basic concepts to keep in mind when you are thinking about compatibility. You want to remember that although Sun sign characteristics describe central and important themes in life, the Sun does not represent the *whole* person. Planets, particularly Venus, are also important to consider when determining compatibility between people. Venus is the planet that symbolizes your concept of an ideal relationship. It describes how you like to give and receive affection. The sign that Venus occupied at the time of your birth explains what is most important to you when you are in love. Other planets are equally important when it comes to relationships: Mercury is the planet that reveals your communication style; Mars is the planet of action and desire. The Moon shows your emotional temperament and security concerns.

Signs that are opposite each other in the zodiac are often compatible, although their personality characteristics are very different. Libra is Aries' opposite sign.

Now, with these considerations in place, we can proceed!

COMPATIBILITY GUIDE

Aries and Aries

You two totally "get" each other; you resonate; you are so much alike. You are both assertive and feisty and like to be on the move planning your next adventure. It is easy to have fun and hard to be bored when you are together.

The challenge: Being overly competitive or having to get your own way can cause this relationship to go up in smoke.

Aries and Taurus

The differences in personality can attract you to each other. You love a Taurus's stable and earthy nature. A Taurus has the loyalty to hang in there with you, and you love knowing you can depend on him or her.

The challenge: A Taurus moves at a slower rhythm than you do. Cultivate patience to make this relationship work.

Aries and Gemini

You love Geminis' playful nature. They are clever, inventive, and have lots of great ideas that make all of your adventures more fun. You both like to kid around and act silly. A Gemini is attracted to your independent spirit.

The challenge: Geminis are communicators, so make sure you slow down and have conversations to make this relationship thrive.

Aries and Cancer

Cancers respond to the world and are motivated to do things by the strength and the passion of their feelings. You know plenty about passion and have a deep understanding of this trait in Cancers. You both know how to step out into the world to follow your dreams.

The challenge: A Cancer's cautiousness is so different from your leap-headfirst-into-life style that you will need to honor this very different approach for this relationship to succeed.

Aries and Leo

Fun and drama are the keywords for this match. Leos are the first to support and understand your creativity. They love your outgoing personality and your sense of adventure. You both like to think BIG and do not let the details hang you up. Leos love a show, so express your love with dramatic flourishes.

The challenge: Since Leos need attention, make sure your adventures don't take you away from spending time together. Be considerate of your Leo's needs to make this relationship grow.

Aries and Virgo

You both aim high and are idealistic and active, although you have different approaches to life. A Virgo brings a grounded, earthy energy to the relationship, which offers a perfect balance to your jump-out-and-do-it style.

The challenge: Virgos like to plan, whereas you are more spontaneous. This relationship needs balance between these two styles for you both to be content.

Aries and Libra

Aries and Libra have opposite approaches to life, which makes them a natural couple. You love the charm, grace, and sociability of this sign. A Libra knows just how to smooth some of your rough edges. Libras are attracted to your assertiveness and enjoy your adventurousness.

The challenge: Although a Libra doesn't mind doing what you want to do much of the time, make sure your Libra's wishes are being considered also to make this relationship work.

Aries and Scorpio

Life is never boring with this match. You each have energy to spare and are both intense and passionate. You will go to the ends of the earth and back for each other. It is a sacred trust when a Scorpio shares his or her heart with you. Here, loyalty and love go together.

The challenge: Scorpios are often more sensitive than they appear and like to take their time getting to know someone. Make sure you don't rush your Scorpio if you want this relationship to flourish.

Aries and Sagittarius

You inspire each other to reach for the stars. Funny and fun to be with, Sagittarius is your adventure pal. Sagittarians are eager to support your dreams and to encourage you to go as far as you can in life. You both are courageous, independent, and idealistic. There is little you cannot do when you are together.

The challenge: You both are so independent that you may have trouble keeping track of each other! Adventuring together instead of independently helps to keep this relationship on track.

Aries and Capricorn

You love and relate to the ambitions of your Capricorn. You both know where you want to go and aren't afraid to take the steps to get there. Neither one of you is a homebody. Capricorns are earthy and practical. They know enough about how the world works to make successful lives.

The challenge: A Capricorn's grounded approach can balance your spontaneity or dampen your enthusiasm. For this relationship to last, you each need to adjust to the other's style.

Aries and Aquarius

Aquarians bring unpredictability and excitement into your life. They come up with adventures that even you haven't thought of before. You both love your independence. The fact that an Aquarius doesn't try to tie you down keeps you coming back for more.

The challenge: As independent free spirits, your travels may eventually take you in opposite directions if you don't make a point to travel together.

Aries and Pisces

You are both dreamers and idealists at heart, so you really connect at a core level. You appreciate a Pisces' sensitivity and compassion. Pisceans admire your go-getter personality. Your different personalities attract you to each other.

The challenge: You are active and impulsive, whereas Pisceans need to make sure something feels right before they act. Adapt to this different way of approaching life to help this relationship prosper.

SPECIAL TIPS FOR ARIES

Below are reminders and special tips that will help any Aries lead a successful and fulfilling life. Maximize your positive traits, and be aware of those traits that can hold you back. Make the effort to learn from your mistakes, and keep your eyes on the stars!

1. Be a pioneer.
2. Go for it!
3. Be assertive, not aggressive.
4. Allow your warrior spirit to motivate you to accomplish great things.
5. Earn more independence by taking responsibility.
6. Set mini-goals.
7. Do not just use your head—use your mind.
8. Go on an adventure or vision quest.
9. Don't bury your anger or throw tantrums. Allow your anger to motivate you to seek solutions.
10. Do not sit around—be active!

You, dear Aries, are a pioneer. Your courage, idealism, and desire to live life to its fullest will lead you into thrilling adventures that are fun and exciting. If you let your enthusiasm motivate you to aim for the stars, there is no dream that you cannot fulfill.

Taurus

The Jewel of the Earth
April 20 to May 21

Symbol: The Bull
Ruling planet: Venus
Element: Earth—*practical, cautious, reliable*
Mode: Fixed—*determined, loyal, stubborn*
Birthstone: Emerald
Colors: Pink and blue

FAMOUS TAURUS PEOPLE:

April 20	Jessica Lange	April 27	Coretta Scott King
April 21	John Muir	April 28	Jessica Alba
April 22	Jack Nicholson	April 29	Michelle Pfeiffer
April 23	William Shakespeare	April 30	Kirsten Dunst
April 24	Barbra Streisand	May 1	Judy Collins
April 25	Renée Zellweger	May 2	Bianca Jagger
April 26	John James	May 3	Sugar Ray Robinson
	Audubon	May 4	Audrey Hepburn

May 5	Tammy Wynette	May 14	George Lucas
May 6	Rubin "Hurricane"	May 15	Brian Eno
	Carter	May 16	Janet Jackson
May 7	Robert Browning	May 17	Debra Winger
May 8	Jean Henri Dunant	May 18	Margot Fonteyn
May 9	Billy Joel	May 19	Lorraine
May 10	Judith Jamison		Hansberry
May 11	Salvador Dalí	May 20	Cher
May 12	Jiddu Krishnamurti	May 21	Peter Hurkos
May 13	Darius Rucker		

THESE BEHAVIORS AND ATTITUDES INCREASE CONFIDENCE

Reliability
Loyalty
Practicality
Patience
Gentleness
Determination
Generosity

THESE BEHAVIORS AND ATTITUDES DECREASE CONFIDENCE

Stubbornness
Resistance to change
Possessiveness
Self-indulgence
Materialism
Controlling tendency
Overcautiousness

THE JEWEL

You, dear Taurus, are a child of the earth. Taurus is the first earth sign of the zodiac, and few have a greater appreciation for all of the beautiful and wonderful things this earth has to offer than a Taurus. Whether it is a colorful sunset, a gorgeous piece of music, or a delicate flower growing by the side of the road, you notice and appreciate many aspects of the physical environment that others pass by or take for granted. You have an unusually high level of attunement to the earth itself. Fittingly, the founding of Earth Day, April 22, 1970, took place and is celebrated each year when the Sun is in Taurus.

Some Taureans are naturally drawn to environmental causes or activities that emphasize nature or the earth. Taurus John Muir was a conservationist who promoted the establishment of national parks. Ornithologist and artist John James Audubon became famous for his paintings of birds.

A Taurus's appreciation of beauty and creativity naturally finds expression in the arts. Painters (Salvador Dalí, Willem de Kooning), singers (Barbra Streisand, Janet Jackson), musicians and composers (Stevie Wonder and Tchaikovsky), actors (Michelle Pfeiffer and Al Pacino), dancers and choreographers (Judith Jamison, Martha Graham), and playwrights (William Shakespeare and Lorraine Hansberry), are all born under artistic Taurus.

Your earthy nature makes you practical and gives you a strong urge to attain material security. Some Taureans are also interested in making earthly living more comfortable and materially secure for others. Taurus Coretta Scott King creates a better world for countless people through her work advocating equality for all human beings. Florence Nightingale improved life for others by founding the nursing profession. Jean Henri Dunant was the Swiss founder of the International Red Cross, an organization that provides practical necessities such as food, medicine, and shelter to victims of catastrophes. Indian philosopher Jiddu Krishnamurti and American philosopher Wayne Dyer address earthly living in still another way. They teach people to create a fulfilling, comfortable, and secure life by combining spiritual and material values.

As an earth sign, you understand that ideas, thoughts, and beliefs need to be practically applied to create a more secure and beautiful world. You are not just a thinker; you are a *doer*.

The Value of Loyalty

No matter where you turn your considerable talents, one thing is for sure: When you invest your attention and energy in something, you will see it through to the very end. Two of your gifts are determination and staying power. You are not a quitter; you finish those things you begin. Your loyalty to a cause, to a person, or to your opinions is one of your best traits. You know how to hold your ground. This is a wonderful quality. It nurtures constancy and lets people know that they can count on you. You do not change sides every two minutes, nor do you decide to do something other than what you promised someone you would do. These are attributes of what is called character. This deep sense of integrity will carry you far in life.

Taurus celebrities are often the ones who have been around for a long time. Cher has been singing for thirty years, and she still makes it to the top of the *Billboard* music charts. Taureans Al Pacino, Barbra Streisand, Shirley MacLaine, and Jack Nicholson are still at the top of their professions after decades. Like these celebrities, you are able to reach your goals because of your strength, determination, stamina, and patience. These qualities will help you lead a successful and rewarding life.

Maintaining Security While Allowing for Change

Sometimes the ability to hang in there until the end may not help you. Although change can be beneficial, it is often hard on a Taurus. A set routine is comforting. You dislike surprises and would rather know ahead of time what is expected of you. Taurus is a very security-focused sign. And, your idea of security may be based on an absence of change. But since life is often unpredictable, when circumstances call for it, although you may feel a bit rattled, it is important for you to find a way to flow with change.

To help yourself approach new situations with a positive attitude, think of a time when you resisted a change that later turned out to be beneficial. Often, it is simply the fact that something is unknown that can cause you to hold back. Cultivating the ability to be adaptable enhances your inner sense of security.

Resistance to change can bring out one of your worst qualities: stubbornness. Watch out for a tendency to refuse to budge or compromise just for the sake of not wanting to change. This tendency to "dig in your heels" can hold you back in life. Know the difference between being purposeful (having a good reason to stand your ground) and being just plain stubborn. There are situations where the ability to be flexible will be a deciding factor in your being successful.

The Material World

Your appreciation for the material world may at times lead to excess: too many cookies, too many clothes, too many belongings, too much of everything! Taureans are known for their appreciation of the finer things in life. You love to experience all of your physical senses—touching, smelling, seeing, hearing, and tasting. The pleasure you take in indulging your senses can cause you to gain weight. Chances are you have a "sweet tooth." There is sweetness in this world—and you know it! Taurus Dennis Rodman, the talented and controversial basketball player, exemplifies self-indulgence, although he is an unusual example of this sign. Most Taureans are more reserved.

Some Taureans, because of their earthy focus, accumulate objects just for the sake of owning them. Taurus talk show host Jay Leno is well-known for his large collection of cars. In a positive sense, you make a great collector and have a fine appreciation of value. You may enjoy collecting coins, baseball cards, stamps, dolls, or other objects. You have an eye for choosing things that increase in value over time. However, if you collect just to have more stuff, you may become material-istic. A great need to possess someone or something can cause difficulties.

Make sure you are not so focused on the material world that you forget about the needs of your soul. Balancing mate-rial values with spiritual values is important for every Tau-rus. Do not allow the sweetness of life and the material pleasures of the earth to lead you away from your inner self.

Taking Your Time

As a Taurus, you know how to pace yourself and take your time. You would think that with all of the hustle and bustle and speeding around feeling stressed and overscheduled, people would appreciate those who have a natural slow, steady rhythm and know how to pace themselves. Instead, folks often want to hurry a Taurus along and get impatient with the slower speed at which a Taurus operates. (As if doing some-thing quickly were better!) The fable "The Tortoise and the Hare" illustrates that rushing ahead and doing things quickly does not necessarily mean that you win the race. In this story, it is the tortoise that crosses the finish line first.

Make sure you hold your ground and go at the tempo that is comfortable for you. Many good things take time to come to fruition, to mature, to flower. Do not allow people who speed through life to rush you. Honor your natural rhythm.

Your Soul Mission: Building a Foundation of Values

Taurus is the sign associated with values. Values are an inner guidance system. They reflect your principles and standards and what you think is worthy and important. Issues of worth also include self-worth. It is important, as a Taurus, to think about and cultivate values that reflect you. Your values form the foundation on which you stand in life.

Taurus Oskar Schindler, whose story was portrayed in Steven Spielberg's film *Schindler's List,* stuck to his values during World War II. In the face of unspeakable horror and danger, he saved many people from the Nazi concentration camps. Taurus Rubin "Hurricane" Carter stood by his values even when imprisoned for a crime he did not commit. Although there are those who disagree with Taurus Shirley MacLaine's spiritual values, it has not stopped her from writing and speaking about their importance in her life.

Think about your own values. What are they? Do they have a central place in your life? Take the time to think about what is important and meaningful to you. Notice if your values help you to make important or even difficult decisions.

Cultivating strong values also requires appreciating yourself. If you know that you are valuable, others will know it, too. If you do not think you are important, others may not either. There is a saying that we teach others how to treat us. Make it a priority to cultivate a strong sense of self-worth. People who know how valuable they are, are more likely to make decisions that lead to happy and successful lives.

FRIENDSHIP

A friend of a Taurus is a friend for life. You are not a "fair-weather" friend. It would take a lot for you to turn away from someone. Loyalty, one of your best traits, is alive and well when it comes to friendships. Your friends know they can count on you. You are reliable, dependable, and available to your friends in times of need. Plus, you are great at giving practical advice! There is little you will not do for your friends. They know this and appreciate this quality in you.

You are not a social butterfly who is interested in developing a variety of social relationships or spending much time with acquaintances. You prefer to invest your time with people you know well. You are likely to be shy or reserved when you first meet people. It takes time for you to feel comfortable with others.

Because it is in a Taurus's nature to be loyal, you may remain friends with someone with whom you no longer have much in common. Your preference in maintaining the status quo instead of seeking change may prevent you from seeking out new friendships that would enrich your life. Move out of your comfort zone periodically to make new friends.

A Taurus's possessiveness may show up in friendships, making it difficult to share your friends. Do not make the mistake of thinking that your friends "belong" to you. Giving them plenty of breathing room strengthens your friendship bonds.

Check out the compatibility guide later in this chapter to see how your friends' Sun signs match up with yours.

HOME LIFE

A stable family life is very important for a Taurus. You like predictability, a set routine, and as little chaos as possible. You like to know ahead of time what is going to happen and what is expected of you. It is important for you to cultivate as much stability as possible within your family life. Some Taureans do this by setting up their own routine, whether by establishing a study schedule or working at an after-school job. If home life is chaotic, getting involved in school activities can help provide structure.

Because Taurus is a sign concerned with values, many Taureans are strongly influenced by their family's values and are more aware than other kids of their family's financial status.

Comfort is the key word when it comes to the requirements for your bedroom. Your bed ought to feel wonderfully comfortable. In general, you should feel secure and cozy and be surrounded by your favorite things. Because of your highly developed sense of beauty and attunement to the aesthetics of your environment, your bedroom should have plenty of pleasing things to gaze upon. The colors should feel soothing and relaxing.

CAREER

Most Taureans appreciate the security of a steady paycheck and a nine-to-five job. For you, stability and security are important factors. You are practical when it comes to your career choices and are willing to work hard. You are loyal to the job and the people with whom you work. Great at looking ahead, you are likely to think of long-term goals: "If I stay with this company, I should be able to significantly increase my income in five years." You are not necessarily seeking to be the boss (although Taureans make great bosses); you are content to work behind the scenes.

You are likely to have a talent for business and for making money. But, don't take a job that doesn't fit you just because it pays well (unless it is part of a long-term goal). If you get sidetracked into just working for money, the years will spin by and you may find that you never expressed your creativity nor found your calling in life. Choose a career that is a good match for your gifts and talents.

Careers in any field that pertains to the earth are perfect for you, whether you study geology, become a forest ranger, or work for the U.S. Environmental Protection Agency (EPA). Because of your natural affinity for money, you may be interested in going into banking, becoming an appraiser or a jeweler, or starting your own business.

As mentioned before, many Taureans have been drawn to the arts, including singer Janet Jackson, actress Annette Bening, and fashion photographer Richard Avedon.

Once you decide on a particular career, make sure you give yourself permission to change your mind if the job you start out with does not end up being as enjoyable as you thought it would.

Although there are many professions to which you may be drawn, one thing is for sure—you have the patience, determination, and perseverance to succeed at whatever you choose.

RELATIONSHIPS

A Patient and Loving Heart

A Taurus is usually not one to dive headfirst into a relationship. You are cautious by nature and would rather take your time getting to know someone. You are most comfortable when there is a clear commitment between you and the person you care for. You seek security and predictability in relationships. Once you have decided that you like someone, you will rarely change your mind. Your legendary loyalty is in full bloom when it comes to your relationships.

Loving to experience all your senses, you have a passionate nature and long to connect with someone. You are loving and affectionate. After all, your ruling planet, Venus, is named after the goddess of love. You also bring practicality to your relationships. You are willing to work through the hard times. You do not leave at the first sign of trouble. Your heart is patient as well as loving. There is little you would not do to help and support your boyfriend or girlfriend. Taurus singer Tammy Wynette's famous refrain "stand by your man" may sound a bit old-fashioned these days, but the sentiment captures perfectly the loyalty of a Taurus's heart.

Stability in a relationship is important to you. You like knowing where you stand. Unpredictability or too many surprises is unnerving. However, because you dislike change, you may stay with someone just because you are used to that person. Taureans need to listen to their hearts and learn to tell if it is time to move on.

One thing every Taurus needs to watch for is the tendency to become possessive in a relationship. When you love someone, you may hold on a little too tightly. Feeling confident of your own value helps you give your boyfriend or girlfriend breathing room.

Although most Taureans are earthy and practical, it is not uncommon for a Taurus to be attracted to those wild, fiery, unpredictable types. They are intriguing and exciting and add sparkle to your more down-to-earth personality. Or, you may be especially intrigued with those intense, smoldering types who keep you on your toes by their complexity and aura of mystery. Other Taureans are drawn to those who are similar to them.

Sign Compatibility

There are some basic concepts to keep in mind when you are thinking about compatibility. You want to remember that although Sun sign characteristics describe central and important themes in life, the Sun does not represent the *whole* person. Planets, particularly Venus, are also important to consider when determining compatibility between people. Venus is the planet that symbolizes your concept of an ideal relationship. It describes how you like to give and receive affection. The sign that Venus occupied at the time of your birth explains what is most important to you when you are in love. Other planets are equally important when it comes to relationships: Mercury is the planet that reveals your communication style; Mars is the planet of action and desire. The Moon shows your emotional temperament and security concerns.

Signs that are opposite each other in the zodiac are often compatible, although their personality characteristics are very different. Scorpio is Taurus's opposite sign.

Now, with these considerations in place, we can proceed!

COMPATIBILITY GUIDE

Taurus and Aries

The differences in temperament and style are what attract you in this relationship. An Aries tends to be impulsive, while you are more cautious. But, you are both strong people and have plenty of passion. An Aries is fun to be with and spices up your life.

The challenge: An Aries craves independence, so leave your sweetie plenty of breathing room for this relationship to last.

Taurus and Taurus

You both are kind, affectionate, and generous. You are definitely on the same wavelength. You relate to each other's earthy nature. There are no mysteries or guessing games here. You understand your Taurus and in turn feel deeply understood and appreciated.

The challenge: Since you both can be stubborn, make sure that you cultivate some flexibility for this relationship to thrive.

Taurus and Gemini

A Gemini, although somewhat unpredictable and changeable, is fun and entertaining. Your Gemini is attracted to your grounded personality, even while encouraging you to move out of some of your old routines. Here, it is the differences in your personalities that attract you to each other.

The challenge: Gemini is the communication sign, so be ready for long conversations for this relationship to grow.

Taurus and Cancer

This relationship feels comfortable right from the start. You both are content to take your time getting to know each other. Your cautious style complements your Cancer's need for emotional closeness. Gentle and affectionate, you easily find a heart connection with each other.

The challenge: Since Cancers respond to the world through their feelings, be sensitive to your Cancer's emotional life to help this relationship feel comfortable.

Taurus and Leo

You both share the attribute of loyalty, so when you two connect, you can create a strong, lasting bond. But, your personal styles are quite different. As an earth sign you are practical and reserved, while your fiery Leo seeks excitement and drama.

The challenge: Since you both tend to be stubborn, you will each need to compromise at times for this relationship to survive.

Taurus and Virgo

This is a harmonious combination. Because you share the element of earth, there is a level of comfort and ease in relating to each other. Your Virgo is sweet and affectionate and understands your needs and desires. You are both interested in making a lasting commitment.

The challenge: Virgos are a little more active than you. Plan activities or projects to work on together to bring you closer to each other.

Taurus and Libra

Libra shares your ruling planet, Venus, the planet of love, so the connection between you is strong. You love a Libra's grace and charm and feel understood and appreciated whether you are having heart-to-heart conversations or just spending quiet time together.

The challenge: The quality of fairness is so important to a Libra that you will have to make sure that your Libra's needs get equal time for this relationship to work.

Taurus and Scorpio

A Scorpio has an aura of mystery that can be quite attractive to you. Scorpios love your loyal and affectionate nature. You both are strong, determined people. Your gentle ways feel comforting to a Scorpio, while you will be led into emotional depths that you didn't even know existed.

The challenge: Because you are both so strong and fixed in your personalities, make a point of cultivating compromise and flexibility so both of you feel supported.

Taurus and Sagittarius

You are attracted to a Sagittarian's outgoing nature and charm. Sagittarians love your loyalty, dependability, and patience. Although very different from each other, your relationship demonstrates how different personalities joining together can add to the fullness and richness of life.

The challenge: For this relationship to bring happiness, leave plenty of room for your Sagittarian's freedom-loving personality.

Taurus and Capricorn

This relationship brings together two souls who know how to appreciate and support each other. You both tend to be serious about love and commitment. This relationship feels comfortable and like it was destined from the start.

The challenge: A Capricorn often takes on responsibilities that may limit the time he or she can spend with you. Accommodate your Capricorn's schedule to help this relationship thrive.

Taurus and Aquarius

The differences attract you to an Aquarius who is likely to keep you on your toes by showing you different ways of looking at and experiencing life. However, you both have the gifts of determination and loyalty, which help to create a strong and lasting bond.

The challenge: Whereas you have a more reserved and conservative personality, an Aquarius likes to challenge the status quo. Be ready to move out of your comfort zone for this relationship to last.

Taurus and Pisces

Two gentle souls come together to create magic. You are both affectionate and find it is easy to express your devotion to each other. Your Pisces is dreamy, sensitive, and psychic. The two of you don't need any words to feel your special connection.

The challenge: You tend to be more practical than a Pisces. Appreciating your Pisces' dreams and ideals helps to create a loving atmosphere and to bring longevity to this relationship.

SPECIAL TIPS FOR TAURUS

Below are some reminders and special tips that will help any Taurus lead a successful and fulfilling life. Maximize your positive traits, and be aware of those traits that can hold you back. Make the effort to learn from your mistakes, and keep your eyes on the stars!

1. Be purposeful rather than stubborn.
2. Appreciate something without having to own it.
3. Take your time. Do not let anyone rush you.
4. Balance material values with spiritual values.
5. Make change your friend, not your enemy.
6. Live by your values.
7. Cultivate self-worth. You are a valuable person.
8. Help make the earth a better and more beautiful place.
9. Move on when it is important for you to do so.
10. Be loyal to yourself.

✳

You, dear Taurus, as a child of the earth, make the world a better, more beautiful place because of your presence. Your value is immeasurable. You demonstrate to others the importance of loyalty and maintaining strong values. Your determination and strength will take you as far as you want to go.

✳

Gemini

II

The Messenger
May 21 to June 21

Symbol: The Twins
Ruling planet: Mercury
Element: Air—*social, communicative, detached*
Mode: Mutable—*adaptable, changeable, restless*
Birthstone: Agate
Color: Yellow

FAMOUS GEMINI PEOPLE:

May 21	Rudolph Isley	May 28	Ekaterina Gordeeva
May 22	Carson Daly	May 29	Melissa Etheridge
May 23	Jewel	May 30	Wynonna Judd
May 24	George Washington Carver	May 31	Walt Whitman
		June 1	Alanis Morissette
May 25	Mike Myers	June 2	Tara Lipinski
May 26	Lenny Kravitz	June 3	Josephine Baker
May 27	Rachel Carson	June 4	Angelina Jolie

June 5	Mark Wahlberg	June 14	Steffi Graf
June 6	Marian Wright Edelman	June 15	Courtney
June 7	Paul Gauguin		Cox Arquette
June 8	Frank Lloyd Wright	June 16	Alice A. Bailey
June 9	Michael J. Fox	June 17	Venus Williams
June 10	Elizabeth Hurley	June 18	Paul McCartney
June 11	Jacques Cousteau	June 19	Paula Abdul
June 12	Anne Frank	June 20	Cyndi Lauper
June 13	W. B. Yeats	June 21	Jean-Paul Sartre

THESE BEHAVIORS AND ATTITUDES INCREASE CONFIDENCE

Adaptability
Quick-wittedness
Inventiveness
Friendliness
Communicativeness
Sociability
Curiosity

THESE BEHAVIORS AND ATTITUDES DECREASE CONFIDENCE

Unreliability
Superficiality
Flightiness
Inconsistency
Moodiness
Gossiping
Opinionatedness

THE MESSENGER

You, dear Gemini, have something to say, to preach, to write, to communicate. You are the messenger: a translator and interpreter of the world. You gather information and then share the news, what's what, the information that helps all of us to have more enjoyable, knowledgeable, and meaningful lives.

Some Geminis speak through their poetry, as did Walt Whitman and W. B. Yeats. Some sing it, like Jewel, Alanis Morissette, and "the godfather of soul," James Brown. Mike Myers and Tim Allen communicate through comedy, and Mary Cassatt and Paul Gauguin expressed themselves through their paintings. Skaters Tara Lipinski and Ekaterina Gordeeva communicate through body language. Some translated the world through their philosophy, like Jean-Paul Sartre, theosophist Alice Bailey, and Methodist Church founder John Wesley.

Geminis are natural-born communicators, although, as you can see by the above list, they communicate in a variety of ways. As an air sign, Gemini responds to the world through the mind, gathering and distributing information. Comfortable in the mental realms, all Geminis are thinkers even if they are quiet—although most Geminis like to communicate out loud.

Mercury: The Messenger of the Gods

Mercury is Gemini's ruling planet. In mythology, Mercury is the traveling ambassador of the gods, carrying messages back and forth between humans and the immortals, and among the gods themselves. Like Mercury, you are highly perceptive and easily make connections between ideas, bridging the gap among worlds, concepts, and people.

In this world there are many Gemini messengers. In 1962, Rachel Carson, an ecologist and marine biologist, wrote *Silent Spring,* which highlighted the effects of pesticides on food and the environment. This book led to a presidential commission and fostered the modern environmental movement. Oceanographer Jacques Cousteau revealed the mysteries of the ocean through his study and photography of undersea life. Anne Frank, who hid from the Nazis for twenty-five months, and eventually died in a concentration camp during World War II, wrote about her experiences in her famous diary. Her story is a powerful message about the horrors of the Holocaust.

The Twins

Geminis are much more sensitive than they appear to be at first glance. Although Gemini is a light, airy sign, its symbol, the twins, represents duality: dark and light, good and bad, day and night, Heaven and Earth. There are many stories that draw on this theme of opposites. Much of your life journey is concerned with learning to work with your twin nature. As a Gemini, you truly dwell in two realms. The Greek myth associated with this sign yields some interesting clues to your inner life.

Castor and Pollux were the twin sons of Zeus, the king of the gods, and Leda. Castor was mortal and Pollux was immortal. These twins were so fond of each other that when Castor died, Zeus took pity on them and let them trade places periodically, switching their mortal and immortal status. Even though one twin was in the heavens while the other was on the earth, they were able periodically to spend time together.

Sometimes you, too, reside in the heavens, your feet never touching the ground. In this state, you know that there is much more to life than your five senses tell you. In this divine place, you write songs and poetry, paint and draw; you dream, meditate, and contemplate. Your intuition flowers, your natural lightness and playfulness have full expression, and a colorful rainbow is always on the horizon.

Other times, when you feel like a mortal with your feet firmly on the earth, it may seem as if a veil obscures the enchanting places you have been, as if clouds have blocked the sunlight. Geminis think, "How can I feel one way this morning and now three hours later I cannot see the magic?"

Many Geminis travel between these two worlds. You have a poetic imagination along with a more rational mind. Both sides desire full expression, and part of being a twin means providing equal time. If you become too logical, your imaginative self will start tugging at you; if your feet leave the ground too often, the powers of rational analysis will nag at you.

You are likely to feel moody or restless when only one part of you is being expressed. Sometimes it may be that the magical, imaginative world is so bright that you do not feel anchored at all in the practical world. Other times, you may be in your logical, intellectual mode. Because thoughts and feelings are a natural complement to each other, your emotions can help you to bridge these two worlds. If you are irritable, it may be an indication for you to listen to your twin.

Variety is the Spice of Life
Flexibility and adaptability are two of your gifts. Change does not scare you. In fact, you welcome change because it makes life more interesting! You are willing to entertain any number of ideas and possibilities. And, although you can be opinionated, you are more than willing to change your mind as new information becomes available. This versatility will help you throughout your life because you are not likely to resist changes that are important and necessary to your growth.

Your love of variety and your desire to seek out new experiences may cause you to take on too much, which can lead to burnout. Be selective about how you spend your time and energy. And, take the time to honor your commitments before you move on to a new project, experience, or relationship. Your strong mind helps you maintain stability and balance while making transitions or seeking change.

Why? Why? Why?
Geminis are curious about and interested in almost everything. "Why is the sky blue?" "How do birds stay up in the

air?" "What is the purpose of algebra?" You have an inquisitive, questioning mind. You love to learn and would love to know the answers to all of life's mysteries.

You are interested in countless topics and are not necessarily concerned with whether or not the subject provides useful information or whether you will ever be able to apply it anywhere in your life. You are simply a curious person. Because of this, you know a little bit about many subjects. You often know just enough to carry on an intelligent conversation with just about anybody on any topic. You can talk about so many different subjects that people may assume that you know more than you actually do!

I Hate to Be Bored!

Geminis hate boredom more than anything else. Most anything you do needs to challenge your mind. In school or at a job, it is always important for you to find something new, different, interesting, and challenging. There is nothing worse than a bored Gemini!

Because your quick, inventive mind likes to be fed information, the repetitious routines of school learning may not always hold your attention. Luckily you have a great imagination, which you can use to make boring school subjects more appealing. Challenge yourself to find something interesting in every subject. Devise word games or trivia questions to keep yourself mentally stimulated.

Make sure that part of every day is devoted to something that interests you—that makes life fun and exciting. Find something inspiring in everything that you do.

A Great Sense of Humor

Geminis have a great sense of humor. Your playful mind can find something amusing in almost anything. You are even able to laugh along with others when they make a funny comment about you. Geminis generally make good mimics and can usually learn other languages easily (or at least fake the accent very convincingly!). Drew Carey's and Joe Piscopo's comedy are good examples of Gemini humor. In fact, a mischievous twinkle in the eyes gives away a Gemini!

Making Your Great Mind Work for You

Sometimes, because you are naturally clever, you may focus on being witty without including the important qualities of wisdom and compassion. Gemini is the first sign of the air element—the element of the mind. And even though you are at home in the world of the mind, it is possible to say a lot of words without really relating to anybody.

The people with whom you are speaking want to be heard, understood, and, more important, want to feel as if their ideas and thoughts count. You have such an incredible ability to communicate. When you combine that gift with sensitivity toward others, you improve all of your relationships.

Gemini is the sign that is associated with the nervous system, and it is easy to find Geminis with delicate nervous systems. When tired, stressed, or overstimulated, you may have a tendency to chatter or to flit from thought to thought. Repetition is a symptom of a stressed-out Gemini. If you find yourself saying the same thing over and over, it is a signal that you need to soothe your nervous system. Meditate, take a relaxing bath, or drink chamomile tea. Too much social stimulation or being too busy can leave a Gemini ungrounded. When you feel scattered, it means you need to slow down, quietly gather your thoughts, and bring them to one place—your center.

The Power of Thoughts, the Power of Words

"I think, therefore I am," said Descartes. This is truly the Gemini motto. What you think and what you say are extremely important. Because your mind is so powerful, pay close attention to your thoughts. Since they influence your actions, note whether they are positive or negative.

Positive affirmations are thoughts, words, phrases, or sentences that are repeated silently or out loud in order to produce a happier or more peaceful state of mind. Angry thoughts lead you deeper into anger, whereas harmonious thoughts bring about contentment. Positive affirmations are used to help break a pattern of negative thinking or to simply stop the useless chattering of the mind. Like Mercury, your mind is a guide that carries messages. Tell your mind where you want it to go, what messages you want it to deliver. It is your messenger; choose wisely the messages you give to yourself and others.

As you decide what and how you want to communicate, be aware of a couple of hurdles to overcome. One of the pitfalls for Geminis is that they can sometimes come across as know-it-alls. In fact, you probably do know more about many topics than do a lot of other people. However, that does not mean you have to let everyone know it! Be sensitive to how people are receiving you.

The other communication hazard for Geminis is the tendency to gossip. Because you are perceptive and pick up so many tidbits of information that other people do not notice, chances are you are going to know things about people that other folks do not. It may be tempting to share these. But gossiping undermines trust, and people assume that if you are talking about others behind their back, you are probably talking about them too. Resist the urge to gossip, and you will build numerous meaningful relationships.

Your Soul Mission: Turning Talk into Action

Because you love to think and communicate, there is a danger that you will be "all talk and no action." Words are prime motivators when they serve a purpose. In fact, thoughts lead to words and then to actions. Your mind can move so quickly, flitting from one idea to the next, that you may not slow down enough to try something out. There are a million creative, innovative ideas out there in the world. How many people actually act upon those ideas? If you live mostly in the world of your mind, you will deprive the world of your genius and brilliance. Take the time to follow one idea or project through to completion. This will cultivate discipline and will provide a strong foundation for fully developing your ideas.

Most Geminis learn new information easily. Some rely on this ability without really applying themselves. For example, you may get good grades on tests for which you barely studied. Imagine what you could accomplish if you actually applied your mind. Many Geminis hold themselves back in life by not fully utilizing the gifts of their mind. Don't flit along on the surface of life. Don't sell yourself short. You are capable of so much more.

FRIENDSHIP

Most Geminis are social and friendly. You are basically a "people person" and enjoy spending time with your friends. They know life is going to get interesting when you are around! You are entertaining, you give great advice, and you are good at helping your friends find solutions to their problems. Your natural adaptability makes it easy for you to go along with others' plans. You are not a person who insists on getting your own way. Your friends are likely to be an eclectic bunch because you find all kinds of people interesting. Chances are, some of your friends may not get along with one another or find much in common. You are the common denominator.

Since you hate to be bored, you are attracted to interesting people who are mentally stimulating and enjoy chatting as much as you do. Activities that provide plenty of opportunities for conversation make it easy to make new friends. Working on the school paper, joining a debate club, or getting involved in the school play are all natural areas for you to explore. Making new friends comes easily when you share similar interests.

Make sure your changeable nature doesn't cause you to change friends so often that you don't give yourself a chance to get to know someone well. Strengthen your friendship bonds by cultivating loyalty and consistency.

Check out the compatibility guide later in this chapter to see how your friends' Sun signs match up with yours.

HOME LIFE

Your natural curiosity about the world begins early in life. Your parents may expose you to a range of ideas or philosophies that open your mind to the sheer diversity in the world. Perhaps your parents encourage you to read or focus strongly on your education. Or, your family may be on the move, exposing you to a variety of experiences through travel. This movement out into the world, whether physical or through your mind, triggers your natural curiosity.

Since Gemini is the sign that is associated with siblings, they may play an important role in your life. If you do not have brothers or sisters, you may form sibling-type bonds with others. You enjoy a familiar and familial experience in your relationships.

Every Gemini needs a bookcase for books and magazines and a place for all of those little assorted knickknacks. You like light and airy environments and need plenty of space to accommodate all of your different interests and projects. A phone in your room is a must so that you can catch up with your friends and have those long, heart-to-heart conversations.

CAREER

Geminis do not usually decide when they are young what they want to be when they grow up. Instead, their natural curiosity is likely to encourage them to experiment with a number of possibilities. Many Geminis pursue more than one career.

The first requirement in choosing any career is to find something that stimulates your active mind and holds your attention. Variety is a must! You will not last long in a job that bores you. Generally, your style is to be on the move rather than sitting behind a desk eight hours a day. You need a fair amount of independence and room to breathe. Self-employment appeals to some Geminis. Others have more than one occupation over their lifetime or may even have two jobs at the same time.

Since you are basically a people person, you may have more fun working with people rather than with things. Education, psychology, or law are a few of the many professions that depend upon good communication skills and the ability to work with others.

Like Mercury, the winged messenger, you may be interested in a job that involves traveling. Gemini journalist and photographer Margaret Bourke-White traveled as the first female war correspondent during World War II. Many Geminis are writers, such as Lillian Hellman, Gail Godwin, and Maurice Sendak. Your people and communication skills can help you in careers that involve anything in public relations, sales, or marketing. Many singers and songwriters, poets, and comedians are Geminis. Because of your gift with languages, you may want to explore becoming a foreign-language interpreter or even an astrologer, whose job it is to interpret and translate symbols. You are the messenger. What do you want to communicate and to whom?

RELATIONSHIPS

Seeking Your Twin Soul

For any Gemini, communication is one of the most important requirements for a good relationship. When you express your thoughts, you are sharing something very sacred about yourself. You like to know what your sweetie is thinking, too. Whether you are exchanging ideas, chatting about your day, or sharing your deepest dreams with each other, conversation is the glue that bonds you with another. If you have to ask twenty questions just to find out what kind of day your boyfriend or girlfriend had, you are most likely in the wrong relationship. The quiet type is not for you!

You have a lighthearted, social, and lively nature that can sometimes be flirtatious. You love someone who knows how to be playful with you and how not to worry if you are chatting with someone else. Possessive types are not appealing to you. In fact, your independence is really important—and you don't even mind if your loved one is the freedom-loving kind, too. You like those active, adventurous, on-the-go types. You are attracted to people who think big, aim high, and have goals and dreams that others would think are impossible.

Geminis love people of different backgrounds. People who follow a different religion or are from another culture or race can be intriguing and attractive. Those with different experiences from yours and who can introduce you to ideas that you have never known about can completely capture your heart. You are not looking for someone who is just like you. Variety is the spice of life as far as you are concerned, so the people who grab your attention are those who are unique, interesting, and smart. If they are funny, make you laugh, and tell a good story, they've hooked you all the way. If someone is attracted to you, he or she is going to have to appeal to both your mind and your heart.

More than anything else, you hate to be bored in a relationship. Commitment scares you sometimes because you are afraid you will lose interest—that the person will not be able to hold your attention. You need someone who is both communicative and mentally stimulating. Life is more fun with someone who knows how to keep you on your toes a little bit. For you, predictability is a romance killer. People who are fascinating and have plenty of variety in their own lives are great matches for you.

Sign Compatibility

There are some basic concepts to keep in mind when you are thinking about compatibility. You want to remember that although Sun sign characteristics describe central and important themes in life, the Sun does not represent the *whole* person. Planets, particularly Venus, are also important to consider when determining compatibility between people. Venus is the planet that symbolizes your concept of an ideal relationship. It describes how you like to give and receive affection. The sign that Venus occupied at the time of your birth explains what is most important to you when you are in love. Other planets are equally important when it comes to relationships: Mercury is the planet that reveals your communication style; Mars is the planet of action and desire. The Moon shows your emotional temperament and security concerns.

Signs that are opposite each other in the zodiac are often compatible, although their personality characteristics are very different. Sagittarius is Gemini's opposite sign.

Now, with these considerations in place, we can proceed!

COMPATIBILITY GUIDE

Gemini and Aries

You both are so mischievous that it is easy to have fun and to connect with each other. An Aries is intrigued by your interesting and somewhat unpredictable nature and loves to act on all of those great ideas of yours. You are attracted to the courageous and daring personality of an Aries.

The challenge: An Aries likes to be active rather than sit around and discuss ideas. Being adventurous with your Aries keeps this relationship alive.

Gemini and Taurus

Here, the differences are what attract you to each other. You love a Taurus's determination, strength, and stability. A Taurus loves your lighthearted nature. Since you love to chat, your Taurus will need to put forth the effort to engage your mind to keep you interested.

The challenge: A Taurus moves at a slower and steadier pace than you do. Accommodate this different style to keep this relationship interesting.

Gemini and Gemini

You are so similar; you are like two peas in a pod. Sharing your ideas and dreams together comes easily, and your playful personalities have a field day with each other. There is such a deep understanding between you that you probably read each other's minds and finish each other's sentences!

The challenge: With so much sameness, you may end up feeling more like siblings or twins than relationship partners. Make an extra effort to keep the romance alive to keep this relationship thriving.

Gemini and Cancer

This is an example where the differences between you can be exciting. The emotional life of a Cancer is especially intriguing to you. Cancers love your social, friendly nature. They benefit by your cool, rational logic, while you gain by opening your heart to the world of the emotions.

The challenge: Although both of you are creative and imaginative, you live in the world of the mind, while a Cancer is at home in the world of feelings. Learn to become comfortable with the differences to help this relationship flourish.

Gemini and Leo

This fire and air combination makes for a fun, lively relationship. Leos are entertained by your playful personality. You love the way a Leo's strength and loyalty anchors and focuses your energy. You bring out the best in each other, creating magic when you are together.

The challenge: You may have so much fun that neither one of you gets serious enough to establish a long-lasting relationship.

Gemini and Virgo

You share the same ruling planet, Mercury, which creates a special bond and understanding. You have deep and stimulating conversations. Although you both are thinkers, you tend to approach life differently, with a Virgo having a more practical approach to life than yours. But, you are likely to find this difference interesting.

The challenge: Too much talking and thinking can get in the way of doing anything. Plan activities to keep this relationship balanced.

Gemini and Libra

Both air signs, you two love to chat and spend time sharing your deepest thoughts and dreams. You understand each other at a profound level. You adore Libra's grace, charm, and diplomatic nature, while a Libra loves how interesting life becomes when you are around. This relationship can feel absolutely magical.

The challenge: You are both friendly and social but may avoid some of the more difficult topics. Make sure you keep all lines of communication open for this relationship to last.

Gemini and Scorpio

You tend to be light and airy, while your Scorpio responds to the world through deep emotions. These differences are likely to be fascinating and spark your interest. You love a Scorpio's intensity, determination, and drive. A Scorpio adores your inventive mind. Life is never boring when you two are together.

The challenge: While you love to discuss, analyze, and chat about the things that interest you, your Scorpio is not interested in that much conversation. You will have to know when to back off for contentment to reign in this relationship.

Gemini and Sagittarius

Sagittarius is your opposite sign and is as fun-loving as you with just as good a sense of humor. You two will always find plenty to talk and laugh about. With a Sagittarius, you had better put on your traveling shoes. They love to be on the go. Independence is important to both of you, so neither one is likely to hold on too tight.

The challenge: Since both of you need plenty of room to breathe, make sure your independent natures do not take you in opposite directions.

Gemini and Capricorn

Capricorns are more serious than you are, but have a dry sense of humor that keeps you laughing and coming back for more. You admire a Capricorn's determination and drive to succeed. Your sparkling personality is like a ray of sunshine for a Capricorn. Here, the differences between you add to the richness of life.

The challenge: Your Capricorn's earthy, grounded nature is so different from your lighthearted personality that you both will have to appreciate these differences for this relationship to succeed.

Gemini and Aquarius

Both air signs, the two of you will never run out of things to talk about. An Aquarius has an unusual and inventive mind that keeps you on your toes. You admire that independent, do-your-own-thing vibe. The two of you are like kindred souls with the deepest understanding between you.

The challenge: Since both of you are most comfortable thinking and talking, make an effort to stay in touch with your feelings to keep this relationship balanced.

Gemini and Pisces

You both are creative, imaginative people, which connects the two of you in a unique way. A Pisces comes from the world of feelings, brings poetry into your life, and is enchanted by your friendly nature. Different approaches to life can make this relationship captivating and fun.

The challenge: With this air/water combination, the two of you are on different wavelengths. A Pisces may not talk as much as you would prefer. Embrace the differences to help this relationship last.

SPECIAL TIPS FOR GEMINIS

Here are some reminders and special tips that will help any
Gemini lead a successful and fulfilling life. Maximize your
most positive traits, and be aware of those traits that can hold
you back in life. Make the effort to learn from your mistakes,
and keep your eyes on the stars!

1. Know that you have something important to tell the
    world
2. Just because you can "wing it" doesn't mean you should.
    Don't waste your inventive, creative mind.
3. Don't gossip!
4. You have a great mind—use it. Choose where you want
    your thoughts to go.
5. When you have something important to do, make sure
    there are no distractions in your environment.
6. Keep in touch with your feelings—they nourish and
    enrich your mind.
7. Follow through on your ideas and finish your projects.
8. Do not bore yourself. Make sure you have plenty of vari-
    ety in your life.
9. Keep your "twin" sides, imagination and logic, in balance.
10. Keep your feet on the ground and your head in the stars.

*

You, dear Gemini, are a messenger. You have something
important to communicate. Use the power of your inventive,
creative mind to succeed in anything that captures your
imagination. Trust your natural curiosity to lead you toward
creating an exciting and satisfying life.

*

Cancer

The Guardian
June 21 to July 23

Symbol: The Crab
Sign ruler: Moon
Element: Water—*sensitive, intuitive, deep feelings*
Mode: Cardinal—*energetic, initiating, active*
Birthstone: Pearl
Color: Silver

FAMOUS CANCER PEOPLE:

June 21	Prince William	June 28	Gilda Radner
June 22	Meryl Streep	June 29	Antoine de Saint
June 23	Frances		Exupéry
	McDormand	June 30	Lena Horne
June 24	Mick Fleetwood	July 1	Liv Tyler
June 25	Carly Simon	July 2	Hermann Hesse
June 26	Chris O'Donnell	July 3	Tom Cruise
June 27	Tobey Maguire	July 4	Louis Armstrong

In astrology, the Moon rules the public's moods and feelings. Research suggests that just as the Moon has an effect on the tides, it also influences people's emotions. Like the Moon reflects the light of the Sun, others see themselves in you and easily make an emotional connection. Cancer Princess Diana captivated people everywhere. People related to her sensitivity, empathy, and deep caring for others. Cancer Bill Cosby's television show was popular. People identified with his depiction of family life. The appeal of Cancer Tom Hanks is his everyman demeanor. He seems as if he could be a member of your own family.

Living in Two Worlds

Your symbol, the crab, is a creature of the sea and of the land. Like the crab, you too have an uncanny ability to travel in two worlds. The oceanic world of emotion and imagination and the earthly world of practical concerns are comfortable and natural realms for you. Many artists of all kinds are born under Cancer, using the world of the imagination as a vehicle for self-expression. Some write to express themselves, like E. B. White (*Charlotte's Web*), Antoine de Saint Exupéry (*The Little Prince*), George Orwell (*Animal Farm*), and Hermann Hesse (*Siddhartha*). Many others, such as Harrison Ford and Liv Tyler, communicate through acting. Some are musicians, like Carlos Santana, Courtney Love, and Beck.

You have another quality that is similar to that of your sign's animal symbol. Like the crab that walks sideways, you too can sidestep. Evasive or indirect behavior occurs when Cancers are not at ease with their decisions. Take the time you need before you act upon your decisions. All Cancers need to feel secure, safe, and comfortable before they move out into the world.

Home Is Where the Heart Is

The crab carries its home on its back. You do the next best thing. You create a comfortable, homey environment wherever you are. Your school locker may be decorated with pictures or items that have personal meaning. Your bedroom is probably filled with objects that have special significance and value to you. It is natural for you to bring along some of your favorite possessions when you leave home for an extended period of time. Objects that spark happy memories help you to feel content and comfortable wherever you happen to be.

Connecting with the Past

Cancers have a special connection to and respect for the past and usually have an excellent memory. Events that have been meaningful to you and people you have loved hold a place in your heart forever. Cancers often keep mementos from the past. You are likely to save such things as an old teddy bear from childhood that has one eye and half its fur, a letter from your favorite aunt, or a rock you found in a lake during a trip with your father eight years ago. Familiar objects connected with happy memories have great sentimental value for you.

This tendency to treasure the past sometimes causes you to have trouble letting anything go. Some Cancers have boxes of old stuff that they just cannot get rid of! Friends from the past may remain your friends today even if you no longer have anything in common. When wonderful memories are connected to a person or object, you may not only have trouble letting them go, but also it may feel difficult to share those people or possessions with others. Be mindful of the difference between appreciation and possessiveness.

It's Just a Phase

Just as the Moon travels through many phases as it waxes and wanes from new Moon to full Moon and back again, Cancers too have a fluid, changing emotional life. Others may find this hard to understand. Your sensitivity and responsiveness to your environment and the people in it mean that you are constantly picking up on the moods and feelings of others. As you experience the emotional climate, you reflect those vibes back out into the environment. You may seem moody or hypersensitive to those around you, but sometimes the feelings you are experiencing are not even your own! Make sure you don't get into the habit of unthinkingly reacting to people and events. Instead, *choose* how you want to respond. Occasionally, you may even need to remove yourself from your environment just to clear your head.

Because Cancers are so perceptive, you get "gut feelings" that are often uncannily accurate. You have an extraordinary instinctual wisdom. It is important for you to pay attention to what your intuition tells you. Sometimes you just *know* something without knowing why you know it.

Too Sensitive or in Touch with Your Feelings?

Cancer is a water sign. Water is the element of the emotional world. You naturally respond to the world through this element, which means you often know more about what you are feeling than what you are thinking. This is appropriate and natural for Cancers.

Cancers are sometimes told that they are "too sensitive." However, your sensitivity is a gift. Stay in touch with, honor, and respect your feelings to keep them flowing. Don't let your emotions freeze up (which keeps you stuck in one feeling) or blocked (which prevents you from knowing what you are feeling). Think of your emotions as being like the waves of the ocean. If they stay fluid and rise and fall like the waves, they are less likely to build up, overflow, and overwhelm you.

Some people are baffled by the power of a Cancer's watery, flowing inner world. If others are uncomfortable with their own emotional life, they certainly will not know what to do with yours! Whether people understand you or not, it is so important for you to honor your feelings because, for a Cancer, they are crucial to the development of self-confidence.

Your Soul Mission: Using the Power of Your Feelings

What do your feelings motivate you to do? Cancer is a cardinal sign, which means it is active. Your dynamic energy loves to be channeled into something. Just as water can spill into cracks and crevices where it is not wanted, your emotions can overwhelm you when they do not have a focus. Listen to your feelings and allow your passion to motivate you. You will then know what is important for you to do.

Cancers Meryl Streep and Tom Cruise pour their emotions into their acting. Meryl Streep is renowned for her ability to demonstrate each feeling and thought her characters experience. Cancers Henry David Thoreau and Pearl Buck used writing to express their emotions. Suzanne Vega and Della Reese sing out their feelings. Gilda Radner communicated through comedy, and Arthur Ashe expressed his passion through sports. It does not matter how you express the power of your feelings, it simply matters that you *do!*

There are tools you can utilize to bring yourself into balance when you are overwhelmed. The vital first step is to trust that your feelings are important enough to feel. The second step is to remember that your feelings will change through the process of experiencing them. Like water that becomes more powerful when stopped by a dam, if you stop yourself from experiencing your feelings, they build up and become stronger.

If you want to get quick perspective, activate the air element, which is the element of the mind. Bring in air by taking ten deep breaths. This exercise helps to stimulate your thinking to produce a more objective state of mind. It is difficult to be mentally detached and emotional at the same time. That is why air-sign people sometimes have a hard time knowing what they are feeling and water-sign people can have a hard time knowing what they are thinking! Breathing fully and deeply can help bring you into balance.

It can also be helpful for Cancers to talk to someone who is detached and can offer some perspective. Air signs in general excel at this, so if you know a Gemini, Libra, or Aquarius, you may want to seek his or her input.

FRIENDSHIP

You love to treat people like family, and friends are no exception. You are likely to have friends whom you have known since you were a small child because you excel at creating lasting bonds with others. It would take a lot for you to turn away from someone you have known for a long time.

Your friends feel and appreciate your compassion and concern for them. If they need something, they know you will be there for them. They know they can count on you. You are protective and will stand up and defend them if they are in trouble. There is little you would not do for your friends.

Because you are protective by nature, make sure you do not turn into a "mother hen" with your friends. You may see yourself as simply being considerate, concerned, and offering helpful advice. Your friends may feel a little claustrophobic. It is important for you to know when you need to back off and give your pals some room.

At times, you may be cautious about making new friends. Cancers usually need to know someone for a while before they feel comfortable letting new people into their circle.

More than anything, Cancers are good, loyal friends. You are great at all of those special, caring touches. You remember friends' birthdays and their likes and dislikes and are considerate of their feelings.

Check out the compatibility guide later in this chapter to see how your friends' Sun signs match up with yours.

HOME LIFE

For most Cancers, family life is very important. The desire to create familial relationships can take many forms. You love to nurture and take care of others, whether it is a family of dolls, younger siblings, friends, or pets. Many Cancers have an affinity for and connection with animals.

There is a baby bird in a book by P. D. Eastman that asks a variety of animals and objects, "Are you my mother?" Like this bird, Cancers wonder, "Where do I belong? Who is my family? What is my purpose?" Whether or not your home life is comfortable, make sure you seek out people who support you, whom you can think of as family, and with whom you feel close.

Take the time to create a comfortable, homey environment. Surround yourself with things that have meaning for you. Keep your favorite book of poetry by your bedside; play music that speaks to your soul; have a container of treasures and gifts from people you love; hang up a beautiful painting or photograph.

CAREER

Your first requirement is to choose a career that *feels* right for you. If it doesn't feel right, it's not for you. Cancers need to trust their instincts. You should also choose something you care about. Your heart needs to be engaged in whatever you do.

As you can see from the list of famous Cancer people earlier in this chapter, Cancers occupy a variety of professions. What they all share is the emotional focus and personal concern that they bring to their career, whether they are leading a nation, as Nelson Mandela has done and the fourteenth Dalai Lama continues to do even in exile, or are entertaining people, as does actor and director Forest Whitaker, who chooses his films based on subjects that are close to his heart.

Any job in which you are taking care of someone or something is perfect for you. An environmentalist taking care of the earth, a doctor caring for patients, a businessperson meeting your consumers' needs, a chef feeding your customers, a veterinarian healing animals, or a police officer who "serves and protects" are all good choices. Public relations and sales of any kind are ideal choices, as you tend to have a pulse on public moods and trends. Because of a Cancer's natural focus on matters of the home and family, professions related to this theme, from real-estate agent to family therapist, are also good choices. Through your great instincts you can "read" people—a talent that helps in any profession. Yours is a particularly imaginative sign, so you may be drawn to the arts.

RELATIONSHIPS

Dancing in the Moonlight

Cancers are romantics. You love a moonlit walk on the beach or spending time in the park holding hands with the one you care for. Often, you don't even need to talk. You are not one who needs to fill in the empty spaces with a lot of chatter. Just sharing your time can be enough. When you are in love, you are so tuned into your partner that you can almost feel what he or she is thinking. Emotional closeness is not only comforting—it is magical.

You don't need a lot of bells and whistles to keep you interested. You can have a great time just hanging out at home with your date, eating snacks and watching a movie on television. The important thing for you is being together. You treasure the person with whom you can safely share your deepest feelings, concerns, and dreams for the future. Your contentment comes from knowing that the person you are with cares about how you feel and is protective of you.

Cancers in general are not looking to play the field. You are more interested in getting together with someone who is interested in a lasting relationship. Because of this, you like to take your time getting to know someone. This is natural for Cancers. It would be uncomfortable for you to rush into a relationship. Many actors who are Cancers are known for their devotion to their mates and loyalty to their families even in a social climate where breakups and divorces are commonplace. Tom Hanks and Meryl Streep are just two of the many Cancer actors whose stable marriages and family lives are as noteworthy as their acting talent.

Cancers love to hold on to all of those little keepsakes that remind them of happy times with their loved ones. A shell from your first walk on the beach, the torn ticket stub from your first date at the movies, the note your boyfriend or girlfriend passed to you in class last year are all treasures for you. No one has to guess about how you feel. You wear your heart on your sleeve by showing your love and appreciation for all that your sweetheart does for you.

Your strong feelings often bring out your nurturing instincts. You naturally want to take care of the person you are with and make sure he or she is happy and content. You are a master at the special touches that show how much you care. Just make sure your nurturing instinct doesn't turn you into your partner's "parent," complete with reminders to dress warmly in cold weather and eat a good breakfast! Find the balance between expressing your love and affection and committing "smother-love." Behaving like a parent could kill your romance!

Sign Compatibility

There are some basic concepts to keep in mind when you are thinking about compatibility. You want to remember that although Sun sign characteristics describe central and important themes in life, the Sun does not represent the *whole* person. Planets, particularly Venus, are also important to consider when determining compatibility between people. Venus is the planet that symbolizes your concept of an ideal relationship. It describes how you like to give and receive affection. The sign that Venus occupied at the time of your birth explains what is most important to you when you are in love. Other planets are equally important when it comes to relationships: Mercury is the planet that reveals your communication style; Mars is the planet of action and desire. The Moon shows your emotional temperament and security concerns.

Signs that are opposite each other in the zodiac are often compatible, although their personality characteristics are very different. Capricorn is Cancer's opposite sign.

Now, with these considerations in place, we can proceed!

COMPATIBILITY GUIDE

Cancer and Aries
Both of these signs have the initiative and drive to accomplish something in the world, although they go about it in different ways. Aries jumps headfirst into life, whereas you need to feel comfortable first. An Aries is fun to be with and definitely keeps you interested and on your toes!

The challenge: An Aries' impulsiveness may be so unnerving at times that you'd rather move on to someone more calming. Enjoy the differences to make this relationship work.

Cancer and Taurus
Comfortable and *cozy* are perfect words to describe this couple. You love Taurus's down-to-earth style. A Taurus is loyal, dependable, and is someone you can count on. Both of you like to take your time getting to know each other.

The challenge: Is there such a thing as too much comfort? As relaxed as you are with each other, you may need to spice things up a little to keep this relationship exciting.

Cancer and Gemini
You operate in the world of feeling while a Gemini is most at home in the world of the mind. A Gemini loves your

compassionate heart; you love Gemini's clever mind. Spending time together brings out the playful, silly side in both of you.

The challenge: Geminis need plenty of stimulating discussions to keep from getting bored. For a Gemini, silence is not golden! Too much quiet time will end this relationship.

Cancer and Cancer

You two totally understand each other. You respond to the world in the same way and have a deep appreciation and sensitivity for each other's feelings. Here, two hearts join in harmony. There is nothing you would not do for each other. This connection feels magical right from the beginning.

The challenge: Sometimes too much sameness can get on your nerves. To keep this relationship on track, don't allow your innate caution to prevent you from confronting conflicts.

Cancer and Leo

Even though you are from different elements (water and fire), you are both passionate and heart-centered. Leos are loyal, strong, fun to be with, and easy to adore. Your nurturing instincts go into overdrive with this one, and your Leo loves every minute of it! This relationship brings plenty of drama into your life.

The challenge: A Leo may not be as sensitive to your feelings as you would like. You will need to keep that in perspective for this relationship to feel comfortable.

Cancer and Virgo

This relationship is as smooth as honey because you have such a profound connection between you. You both are content to take your time getting to know each other. Neither of you is in a rush. This relationship can go as deep as you want it to go.

The challenge: Although a Virgo's analytical nature is focused on improvement, it sometimes comes out as criticism. Make sure you let your Virgo know if he or she crosses that line.

Cancer and Libra

You are both compassionate and sensitive. You are more centered in your emotional life than is a Libra, but you both come from the heart. Here, it is the differences that attract you. Neither of you really likes to make a fuss; you instead focus on ways of remaining close to each other.

The challenge: Both of you have a tendency to avoid conflict, which can prevent you from discussing important matters concerning your relationship. You will need to find a way to talk about your problems for this relationship to work.

Cancer and Scorpio

It is easy to feel supported by a Scorpio. You are both oriented in the world of emotions and understand and respect the other's tender heart. Passion runs high in this relationship, and the intensity of your feelings for each other is strong. You both have staying power and are looking to make a deep, lasting connection.

The challenge: Scorpios are generally more private than you are, being slow to open up. You will need to respect your Scorpio's pace for this relationship to flourish.

Cancer and Sagittarius

Sagittarians are exciting and fun to be with. They love to explore the world—so it may be hard to find them at home! With this match, the differences attract, providing you both with different perspectives. Your Sagittarius is a great cheerleader for you and the first to encourage you to go for your dreams.

The challenge: Because you prefer emotional closeness, the independent needs of a Sagittarius may be uncomfortable for you. You will have to give your Sagittarius plenty of room for this relationship to thrive.

Cancer and Capricorn

Capricorn is your opposite sign, which creates a natural attraction. You love the strong, self-sufficient energy that emanates from a Capricorn. Both of you are cautious and reserved by nature and interested in making a lasting commitment.

The challenge: A Capricorn's earthy, practical, and at times cynical take on life is very different from your feeling-oriented focus. Appreciation of this difference will bring you closer to each other.

Cancer and Aquarius

Aquarians make life interesting by bringing different ways of looking at and experiencing life. You are intrigued by that independent do-your-own-thing style. With an Aquarius you will never be bored. You are both passionate people who care deeply not only for each other, but also about the well-being of others.

The challenge: Aquarians tend to be detached and logical with a strong need for independence, which can clash with your need to be emotionally close. Give your Aquarius a lot of room to help this relationship grow.

Cancer and Pisces

You two can be positively psychic with each other! Often, words are unnecessary, since you are so tuned into your Pisces and your Pisces into you. Both of you are naturally affectionate, romantic, and sensitive to each other's feelings. A Pisces loves to help, give to, and connect with you.

The challenge: You both tend to be sensitive and will need to be careful not to tread on the other's emotions. Make sure you talk about your feelings to keep this relationship flowing.

SPECIAL TIPS FOR CANCERS

Below are reminders and special tips that will help any Cancer lead a successful and fulfilling life. Maximize your positive traits, and be aware of those traits that can hold you back. Make the effort to learn from your mistakes, and keep your eyes on the stars!

1. Honor and respect your feelings.
2. Allow your emotions to flow like the waves of the ocean.
3. Give people the space they need.
4. Sit under the moonlight at least once a month and focus on your dreams.
5. Make sure that you are not just looking after others, but also taking care of your own needs.
6. If people do not understand you, it does not mean they do not love you.
7. You have great instincts. Trust them!
8. Don't get waterlogged; express yourself.
9. Allow your passions to motivate you to do something.
10. Don't rush. Take the time you need to feel comfortable with your decisions.

$*$

You, dear Cancer, are a guardian with deep, tender feelings, a compassionate heart, and a great imagination. Your feelings will guide you in creating the life you desire. The world will be a better place because of who you are and what you do.

$*$

Leo

♌

The Leader

July 23 to August 23

Symbol: The Lion
Sign ruler: Sun
Element: Fire—*outgoing, enthusiastic, strong*
Mode: Fixed—*determined, loyal, stubborn*
Birthstone: Ruby
Colors: Yellow, orange, and gold

FAMOUS LEO PEOPLE:

July 23	Woody Harrelson	July 31	Wesley Snipes
July 24	Amelia Earhart	August 1	Herman Melville
July 25	Matt LeBlanc	August 2	James Baldwin
July 26	Sandra Bullock	August 3	Martha Stewart
July 27	Peggy Fleming	August 4	Raoul Wallenberg
July 28	Beatrix Potter	August 5	Neil Armstrong
July 29	Paul Taylor	August 6	Lucille Ball
July 30	Lisa Kudrow	August 7	David Duchovny

August 8	Isabel Allende	August 16	Madonna
August 9	Whitney Houston	August 17	Robert De Niro
August 10	Antonio Banderas	August 18	Robert Redford
August 11	Alex Haley	August 19	Matthew Perry
August 12	Cecil B. DeMille	August 20	Connie Chung
August 13	Alfred Hitchcock	August 21	Wilt Chamberlain
August 14	Halle Berry	August 22	Tori Amos
August 15	Ben Affleck	August 23	Kobe Bryant

THESE BEHAVIORS AND ATTITUDES INCREASE CONFIDENCE

Determination
Confidence
Creativity
Leadership
Generosity
Kindness
Respect

THESE BEHAVIORS AND ATTITUDES DECREASE CONFIDENCE

Showing off
Arrogance
Stubbornness
Disrespectfulness
Bossiness
Controlling tendency
Rigidity

LEADERSHIP

Just as your sign ruler, the Sun, is at the center of the solar system, you, too, have a life where you are often at the center. People notice when you walk into a room. You have charisma, that special quality that attracts people's attention. This is true if you are the more outgoing, extroverted kind of Leo like Mick Jagger, Jennifer Lopez, or Madonna, or a more reserved type of Leo like David Duchovny, Robert Redford, or Sean Penn. The more reserved Leos have just as much presence and are just as noticeable as the more outgoing ones.

Your symbol, the lion, is known as the king of the jungle, and Leo is the sign of leadership. Leadership takes many different forms. Some Leos like to run their own businesses, such as Martha Stewart, who virtually has a home-and-lifestyle empire. Paul Taylor started his own dance company. Movie star Arnold Schwarzenegger was appointed fitness czar by former president George Bush to encourage people to exercise. Many Leos become leaders in their profession, such as Lucille Ball (comedy), Robert De Niro (acting), and Beatrix Potter (children's books). Leos naturally gravitate toward being the one in charge. You have the desire and the ability to be the leader of the pack.

Strength and determination are two of your gifts and provide an excellent foundation for your leadership. You can move mountains with your strength. You naturally take charge of any situation in which you find yourself. Usually others are happy to let you assume this role. But, when others do not want to go along with your plans or take your advice, watch out for your tendency to be bossy. Because you have such a strong sense of authority, you may think you know what is best for others. Although you often give excellent advice, make sure it is requested. Getting your own way is less important than you sometimes believe.

You give your heart and soul to whatever you do. You don't like to do anything halfway: It's all or nothing. This trait helps you achieve your goals. Others may want to reach the top of their class, sport, or profession, but you actually do the hard work that is necessary to get there. There is a reason that Leos end up in leadership positions. It is because they have demonstrated that they are capable of leading!

Many Leos are high achievers and great organizers. Working hard, doing your best, and setting high standards are some of your greatest strengths. There is a perfectionist in every Leo. If you prepare a dish to take to a party, you make sure it is the most original, incredible, best-tasting dish that anyone has ever seen. If you design leaflets for an event, you make sure they are a work of art. You show off your creations proudly and wait for the applause to follow. And often you do get great feedback. But, even though others' appreciation is wonderful, it is important for you to be your own audience. Feeling great about what you do is the best feeling.

The Gift of Courage

Courage is one of your gifts. Many Leos are famous for having the courage of their convictions. Their bravery causes them to do things that others would not even consider. During World War II, Swedish diplomat and businessman Raoul Wallenberg helped 100,000 Hungarian Jews escape deportation to the concentration camps. Astronaut Neil Armstrong was the first person to set foot on the Moon. Amelia Earhart was the first woman to fly across the Atlantic Ocean. Julie Krone entered the male-dominated field of horse racing and became the only female jockey to win a Triple Crown race and the only woman to be inducted into the National Racing Hall of Fame.

Do you take chances? What is your passion? Make sure you explore the activities that you love. Your courage is there to help you follow your dreams. Be confident and loyal to your convictions, and you will create a fun and interesting life.

The Tender Heart behind the Lion's Roar

When a Leo gets upset or is not properly respected, the normally magnanimous king or queen of the jungle can let out a roar that would scare anybody! But that bellow covers a tender heart. You are, in spite of all appearances, a sensitive and often shy person. You tend to let your strength and determination carry you, hiding your softer side. Remember, you don't have to be strong all of the time. By allowing others to see all of you instead of just the part that is in control, you will not only improve your relationships, but you will feel more balanced. Strength is ultimately enhanced by sensitivity.

The World Is Your Playground

All Leos need to have fun. While that's true for everybody, for Leos it is a necessity. Which activities feed your spirit, make you glow, and make life fun? Make sure you do something fun every week. See the world as your playground. What do you want to create, to express? Part of becoming a confident Leo is knowing how to have fun.

For some Leos, having fun is the same thing as being creative. Many Leos are exceptionally imaginative. Performers of all kinds were born under this sign. But creativity is not only about performing. Creativity is the act of creating something, whether it is a work of art, a new scientific concept, or a heart-surgery technique. Creativity is simply the act of expressing yourself, of communicating what is inside you. Leos Isabel Allende and J. K. Rowling communicate through writing. Peggy Fleming expresses herself through figure skating. Alfred Hitchcock directed movies. Henry Ford's passion was automobiles. He founded the Ford Motor Company. Alexander Fleming's interests led to him to discover penicillin. All of these Leos expressed their creativity and followed their passion. What is fun for you? When Leos have fun, they spark their creativity and increase their confidence—and people notice them.

I've Got to Be Me

The most important thing in the world is to simply be yourself. It is interesting to note that Leo is the sign that is associated with children. Young children are perfect examples of Leo energy at its purest. They know how special they are— not because they have to prove anything or work hard, but just because of who they are. A child delights in drawing a picture with colorful crayons for others to admire. People share this delight and put that picture on the refrigerator for everyone to see. This childlike enthusiasm about one's own creativity is one of your gifts and holds the key to your own confidence. Something in you knows how special you are, and that you don't need to prove it to anybody.

Your task is to be yourself—to be your radiant, majestic self. Express what you want to express, not what others want for you. Have faith in yourself. Respecting your own uniqueness strengthens you and builds your confidence. When you shine like the Sun, people turn toward you to bask in your warmth, your light, and your generosity.

Developing Self-confidence

How does the Leo vibe, that compelling sense of authority and presence, develop? The answer to this question is the journey of every Leo.

Leos, even the more outgoing ones, often talk about feeling a lack of self-confidence when they were young. Though most Leos know in their hearts that they are special, they can have a hard time just being one of the crowd and feeling like they fit in. This sign is concerned with the *journey* to self-confidence, about the *process* of becoming a leader. There are steps you can take toward becoming a confident person, establishing your authority, and becoming the center of your own solar system.

Leos like to experience a fair amount of control. You need something to be in charge of, something you do extremely well and that gives you a sense of accomplishment and authority. This "something" should be tangible and specific. When you think, *I am somebody,* what does that mean to you? What is your "thing"? For some Leos, an after-school job provides a feeling of accomplishment and some control over their destiny. For others, academic achievement promotes confidence. Other Leos join the drama club or the football team and excel in those activities. What is important for every Leo is to find your own special thing. Discover what it is that you love, that you feel you do well. And then put your heart and soul into achieving excellence in your chosen activities. Soon, you will experience the confidence that is the birthright of every Leo.

Your Soul Mission: Giving and Earning Respect

A central question for every Leo is "Do people respect me?" You are sensitive to how people treat you and respond to you. Nothing turns you off more than when you feel someone's lack of respect. And although you rarely show it, your feelings are easily hurt by a person's lack of regard for you. There is a saying, "Respect is earned." This is a good motto for you to keep in mind. Part of every Leo's journey is learning that when you give others the same respect that you desire for yourself, others will be more considerate of your dignity and your feelings. Ask yourself, What have I done or how do I behave that warrants others' consideration? Have I earned their respect?

Approval is also important for any Leo. Although it feels great to bask in the warmth and appreciation of others, do not base your self-esteem on being the center of someone else's solar system. Reside in the center of your own solar system. Feel confident about yourself. If you are comfortable in your own center, you will not be easily pulled offtrack if others do not recognize how wonderful you are.

FRIENDSHIP

Many of the Leo descriptions in astrology books would have you think that you are the life of every party and at the center of every group. Instead, many Leos are more likely to wonder how they fit in with a group. Although some Leos are extroverted and gravitate toward the life-of-the-party role, most Leos have a few close caring friends—often those whom they have known for a while.

You are a warm and generous friend, and there is little you would not do for those you care for. Loyalty to others is one of your best traits. Your friends know they can count on you. This kind of allegiance helps you to form lifelong friendships. But, if a friend betrays you, it may feel impossible to work things out. You have a strong code of ethics and clear-cut standards of right and wrong. This code helps you form an effective foundation in life, but it can also cause you to be rigid. If you leave room in your own heart for the mistakes of others, they may leave room in theirs for yours.

Check out the compatibility guide later in this chapter to see how your friends' Sun signs match up with yours.

HOME LIFE

Many Leos stand out in some way in their families. It may be because of your achievements or your rebellion; it may be because you are an only child, or the oldest child. Or, possibly your parents or siblings count on you in some way. Leo children tend to get attention for some reason. As family members pay attention to Leos, Leos focus on themselves. This is the seed of your lifelong concern with the need to express yourself. The attention you receive can feel great, or sometimes it may feel like pressure—as if you have to perform or do well to keep getting the attention. If you are not getting positive attention, you may act out negatively. If this is happening, it is important for you to find an outlet for your creativity, something to excel in, or something that helps you to realize how great you are. Even within your family life you are learning how to express your own authority and to garner control over your life.

The issues of perfectionism and need for approval evolve from the family atmosphere. Your parents may see great things for you and you naturally want to measure up. Or, one of your parents may be a high achiever and you want to follow that parent's footsteps.

For a Leo, your home is your castle, so you prefer to have some say about what is in your "castle." Display those objects that you love and that say something important about you. Your bedroom—or your part of the room if you share your bedroom—needs to have something that expresses your uniqueness.

CAREER

All jobs that are or lead to authority positions are great choices. You are comfortable being in charge. Your natural tendency to excel, your high standards, and your desire to do a great job set an example for others. In fact, it upsets you if you have not done a task as perfectly as you can. Those in authority notice your willingness to give a job your all and often end up supporting your goals. For example, you may start out waiting tables, then be promoted to manager, and eventually open your own restaurant. People would support your restaurant because of your previous history. They would have confidence in you.

Your career should be fun and should provide an environment in which you can shine and show off what you can do. A job where you are visible is perfect, such as a teacher in front of the classroom, a conductor of an orchestra, or the head of your own software company. Many Leos gravitate to the performing arts. Becoming an actor like Leos Angela Bassett, Hilary Swank, or Matthew Perry; a director like Stanley Kubrick or Cecil B. DeMille; or a singer like Whitney Houston or Jennifer Lopez are choices that are likely to interest you.

Because it is so important for you to feel respected, make sure you do not stay in jobs where you are not treated well. But, also make sure you are earning respect and not just expecting it. In general, Leos have great loyalty to a job. You will tend to stay in your chosen line of work and particular job for a long time rather than flit from career to career. Your gifts of determination and reliability will take you far in your chosen profession.

RELATIONSHIPS

To Love and Be Loved

Leo is the sign of love, making Leos natural-born romantics. You are tender, generous, and passionate; you are strong and kind. You love to be in love, and there is little you would not do for the one you adore. You create pure magic in your relationships. When you feel loved, all is right with the world.

Although you love to be courted and to be the object of someone's affection, you especially love to be the one doing the courting and making the grand, dramatic gestures. Love is not a little thing to you. You like to declare your everlasting love like some character out of a Shakespeare play.

You are idealistic in your relationships and don't like to waste your time or energy on what you consider minor problems. You are fiercely protective and will fight for your loved one's honor. You do not want to hear anything negative about people you care for, even if it's true! Not much is halfway with you, so when you love, you give your whole heart, and your sweetheart has your total loyalty.

Since respect is a key theme for a Leo, you must feel respected and appreciated by your loved one, or the relationship will soon end. The person you care about needs to understand how sacred it is when you give your heart, and needs to treat you accordingly.

There are a couple of factors to keep in mind when you are making decisions about relationships. Watch out for a sweet-talking person who has all the right words. You may be so flattered by the attention that you do not consider who is doing the flattering.

Because of your loyalty and the fixity of your nature, you can stay too long in a relationship that doesn't feel comfortable to you. It may be difficult for you to accept that you have made a poor choice. When a relationship is no longer right for you, make sure you take the steps to move on from the relationship and on with your life.

Sign Compatibility

There are some basic concepts to keep in mind when you are thinking about compatibility. You want to remember that although Sun sign characteristics describe central and important themes in life, the Sun does not represent the *whole* person. Planets, particularly Venus, are also important to consider when determining compatibility between people. Venus is the planet that symbolizes your concept of an ideal relationship. It describes how you like to give and receive affection. The sign that Venus occupied at the time of your birth explains what is most important to you when you are in love. Other planets are equally important when it comes to relationships: Mercury is the planet that reveals your communication style; Mars is the planet of action and desire. The Moon shows your emotional temperament and security concerns.

Signs that are opposite each other in the zodiac are often compatible, although their personality characteristics are very different. Aquarius is Leo's opposite sign.

Now, with these considerations in place, we can proceed!

COMPATIBILITY GUIDE

Leo and Aries

Aries people share your idealism, and you find their outgoing personality and adventurousness fun to be around. You both like to think BIG and do not let the details hang you up. An Aries likes to be on the go, so put on your traveling shoes and get ready to have fun.

The challenge: These two fire signs spark a whole lot of fire! You both are strong and like to get your own way. Compromise will keep this relationship on track.

Leo and Taurus

You are both passionate and loyal, so when you two connect, you can create a strong, lasting bond. Your personal styles are quite different. A Taurus is practical and has his or her feet on the ground. You tend to be idealistic and fiery in your temperament.

The challenge: Since you are equally stubborn, you will both need to become more flexible for this relationship to survive.

Leo and Gemini

This fire-and-air combination makes for a lively and playful relationship. A Gemini is thoroughly entertained by you and loves your generous, giving spirit. Life is fun but unpredictable when a Gemini is in your life. The two of you bring out the best in each other, creating magic when you are together.

The challenge: You may be having so much fun that neither one of you gets serious long enough to establish a long-lasting relationship.

Leo and Cancer

You both are passionate, creative people. A Cancer is tender, compassionate, understands your deepest feelings, and helps you nurture your grandest dreams. Your strength and loyalty is appealing to a Cancer.

The challenge: A Cancer is at home in the world of feelings, which is not the most comfortable world for you. You will need to accommodate this different approach to life to help this relationship thrive.

Leo and Leo

Fun and drama are the keywords for this match! The two of you easily make a heart-to-heart connection because you have such a deep understanding of each other. With this combination, your passion either turns up the heat or burns each other up—sometimes a little of both.

The challenge: Two Leos are like two Suns in the same solar system. Both strong, determined, and liking to lead, you will need to compromise and take turns getting your own way for this relationship to succeed.

Leo and Virgo

Although you two have different temperaments, in many ways those differences can create compatibility. You like to lead; a Virgo loves to support your goals and dreams and won't fight you for the limelight. You love how a Virgo's soothing presence helps keep you calm and your feet on the ground.

The challenge: A Virgo is much more practical than you are and pays attention to things you never even notice. You will need to appreciate this quality to help this relationship along.

Leo and Libra

You share an idealistic nature and are romantics at heart. Both of you love the grand, dramatic declarations of love, which adds to the passion in this relationship. A Libra's gentle and diplomatic nature brings beauty and harmony into your life. You bring fun, drama, and a zest for life that a Libra loves.

The challenge: Libras are naturally tuned into others' needs. Pay attention to your Libra's needs to keep this relationship strong.

Leo and Scorpio

This water/fire combination sizzles! You love a Scorpio's magnetic intensity and mystery. You both are passionate and loyal, which creates a strong connection between you. This is an all-or-nothing combination, since neither of you does anything halfway.

The challenge: Since you both tend to be stubborn, you will have to learn to compromise to help this relationship flourish.

Leo and Sagittarius

Life is fun, dramatic, and always an adventure when you are with a Sagittarius. Both fire signs, you are passionate about life and about each other. You each have big ideas about where you are going in life, and, with each other's support, it will be easy to fulfill your dreams.

The challenge: You two know how to have a good time together. One of you (probably you, Leo) will have to keep a foot in reality to take care of the practical details of living.

Leo and Capricorn

Although your personalities are different, you share an aura of authority and strength that is like a magnet to you both. Committed and passionate about love, you cherish your time together. A Capricorn helps you keep your feet on the ground, and your idealism inspires a Capricorn to reach for new heights.

The challenge: Creating a combination of work and fun, of seriousness and playfulness, will keep this relationship strong.

Leo and Aquarius

Aquarius is your opposite sign, and since "opposites attract," this creates compatibility. You are drawn to an Aquarian's highly original do-your-own-thing personality and appreciate his or her strong streak of independence. An Aquarius loves your warmth and generosity. The differences in your temperaments naturally complement each other.

The challenge: You both are strong, determined, and like to get your own way. Flexibility is the key to making this relationship work.

Leo and Pisces

A Pisces brings enchantment into your life, along with a psychic vibe that is out of this world. You love your Pisces' soothing, gentle touch, and your Pisces basks in your warmth and generosity. Both tenderhearted and big dreamers, you can bring out the best in each other.

The challenge: A Pisces is comfortable in the emotional world, which is very different from your decisive, action-oriented personality. Appreciating your Pisces' sensitivity will help this relationship thrive.

SPECIAL TIPS FOR LEOS

Here are some reminders and special tips that will help any Leo lead a successful and fulfilling life. Maximize your positive traits, and be aware of those traits that can hold you back. Make the effort to learn from your mistakes, and keep your eyes on the stars!

1. Play!
2. Be yourself rather than someone else's idea of who you are.
3. Make changes when necessary.
4. Earn respect; don't demand it.
5. Engage in activities that increase your confidence.
6. Let others see your tenderness and kindness.
7. Find and do something you love and in which you can excel.
8. Don't allow your high standards to turn into perfectionism.
9. Step into leadership roles whenever possible.
10. Be loyal to yourself as well as to others.

You, dear Leo, are a leader. By becoming a confident Sun in your own solar system, you will inspire everyone you meet with your warmth, generosity, and loyalty. With your strength and determination, there is little in life that you cannot achieve.

＊

Virgo

♍

The Practical Idealist
August 23 to September 23

Symbol: The Virgin
Ruling planet: Mercury
Element: Earth—*practical, cautious, reliable*
Mode: Mutable—*adaptable, changeable, restless*
Birthstone: Sapphire
Colors: Blue and gray

FAMOUS VIRGO PEOPLE:

August 23	River Phoenix	August 31	Richard Gere
August 24	Macaulay Culkin	September 1	Gloria Estefan
August 25	Claudia Schiffer	September 2	Salma Hayek
August 26	Mother Teresa	September 3	Marguerite
August 27	Samuel Goldwyn		Higgins
August 28	Shania Twain	September 4	Richard Wright
August 29	Charlie Parker	September 5	Raquel Welch
August 30	Cameron Diaz	September 6	Rosie Perez

September 7	Chrissie Hynde	September 16	Trisha Yearwood
September 8	Jonathan Taylor Thomas	September 17	Phil Jackson
		September 18	Jada Pinkett Smith
September 9	Adam Sandler		
September 10	Ryan Philippe	September 19	Jeremy Irons
September 11	Harry Connick Jr.	September 20	Sophia Loren
September 12	Barry White	September 21	Stephen King
September 13	Milton S. Hershey	September 22	Eric Stolz
September 14	Margaret Rudkin	September 23	Jason Alexander
September 15	Oliver Stone		

THESE BEHAVIORS AND ATTITUDES INCREASE CONFIDENCE

Analysis
Kindness
Insight
Practicality
Observation
Idealism
Dependability

THESE BEHAVIORS AND ATTITUDES DECREASE CONFIDENCE

Criticism
Judgmental tendency
Subservience
Fussiness
Passivity
Self-deprecation
Narrow-mindedness

THE PRACTICAL IDEALIST

You, dear Virgo, are a wonderful combination of idealism and practicality. These qualities serve as a balance for each other to help you achieve your dreams. Your idealistic nature makes you want to achieve nothing less than perfection. The part of you that is practical knows how to devise a plan to reach your goal. Virgos are so often successful in life because they are the people who not only have ideals and dreams, but, more important, also know how to fulfill them.

Virgo Maria Montessori, a pioneer in education and the first woman to receive a medical degree from the University of Rome, created a method of education based on a child's natural development. Although her idealism prompted her to invent this progressive form of education, the Montessori method was based on her real-life experiences in the education of children. She used her common sense; she saw what worked.

English philosopher John Locke's ideals established him as one of the most important thinkers of the modern world. His revolutionary ideas strongly influenced political thought, including the writing of the American Declaration of Independence.

Many entrepreneurs are Virgos who create successful businesses with their combination of idealism and practicality. Some Virgos who created their own businesses are Harland "Colonel" Sanders, J. C. Penney, Margaret Rudkin (the founder of Pepperidge Farm bakery), and Milton S. Hershey (the chocolate manufacturer).

This world is not a mystery to a Virgo. Some people learn how the world operates when they are older. You already know many things that others don't. You observe, you analyze, and you learn. You see what works and what doesn't. This incredible ability to keep your feet on the ground while exploring and developing your ideals and dreams is a gift that will help you go anywhere you want in life.

Practice Makes Perfect

Hard work does not bother you. You are a realist when it comes to achieving your goals. In fact, many Virgos enjoy professions that require effort and time in order to hone and perfect their skills. Renowned figure skater Scott Hamilton put in many hours of hard work to win an Olympic gold medal. Arnold Palmer developed his natural talent by practicing to become a great golfer. Journalist Marguerite Higgins tackled the difficult task of reporting about the Korean War. She became the first woman to receive the Pulitzer Prize for foreign coverage. All of these Virgos took what they loved to do and then became some of the best in their chosen fields.

Virgos enjoy cultivating skills and developing expertise. While many others shy away from what it takes to pursue a dream, you are realistic about the dedication required to reach your goals. You are self-sufficient, amazingly capable, and able to do just about anything you put your mind to.

Virgos are often the ones who so excel at what they do that they are considered some of the best in their genre. For example, Stephen King is a best-selling author of horror fiction. Michael Jackson's talent for singing, songwriting, and dancing puts him in a class all by himself. Magician David Copperfield is at the top his profession. Each of these Virgos applied themselves to become the best at what they do.

Virgos need something to do. You love to be productive and useful. At your happiest, what you do has meaning and purpose for you. By investing your time and energy in the tasks that are the most important to you, you will begin to develop the expertise that leads to a successful life.

Although there are plenty of well-known Virgos, many are naturally reserved or shy. You are not one to clamor for the spotlight. It's not as if you don't like your hard work to be noticed, but your purpose in doing something is that you want to do it—not that you are seeking an audience. You are comfortable working quietly on a project by yourself; you enjoy time spent alone. Although you are fine in big crowds or around a lot of people, in general you are not a "party person," and instead are content to seek the company of a few close friends.

The Gift of Discernment

One of your greatest gifts is your ability to discriminate between what is important and worthy of your attention and what is not. Your flair for determining what has practical value is one of the keys to your success. Many people are held back in life simply by their inability to accurately assess any given situation. Your excellent mind, talent for analysis, and sterling clarity help you to make decisions that are invariably workable.

This gift of discernment blossoms when you give it specific application. For example, Phil Jackson, a great NBA basketball coach, uses his Virgo gifts to bring out the best in each of his players. He recognizes the specific strengths of each player and utilizes those skills accordingly. There are many situations in life where this ability will bring you excellent results.

The Virgin

The term *virgin* is used to signify something that is in its pure state or is untouched or uncorrupted. Virgin wool is unprocessed wool. Virgin oil is oil that is made from the first pressing of olives and is obtained without the use of heat. The Virgo symbol, the virgin, does not signify sexual virginity, but instead represents a person who is self-contained and belongs to no one but her- or himself. This person is considered untouched by others and pure in nature. In this sense, the virgin implies a psychological state of being inwardly focused and not dependent upon others for a feeling of wholeness. The virgin represents the union of body and soul, of spirit and matter. This is a powerful symbol because it represents people who are self-possessed and who lead their lives as they choose rather than following the dictates of others.

It is interesting that in the sign of the virgin are people
who are considered some of the most physically attractive in
Western popular culture: Claudia Schiffer, Sean Connery,
Ingrid Bergman, Shania Twain, Cameron Diaz, Richard
Gere, Salma Hayek, and Sophia Loren.

How Can I Serve?

The pure meaning of service is simply the sincere desire to
help others. This concept has long been associated with
Virgo. Jane Addams, a pioneer in the field of social work,
typifies the Virgo impulse to help people. Her distress at the
conditions of the poor in Chicago led her to create Hull
House, a center that housed a day nursery and kindergarten
and cared for sick and hungry people. In the typical manner
of the Virgo practical idealist, Addams became a garbage
inspector just so she could get the filthy streets cleaned.
Among her many accomplishments were campaigns that
helped pass legislation to prevent the operation of sweatshops
and establish the world's first juvenile court. She was
awarded the Nobel Peace Prize in 1931.

·Virgo actor Richard Gere is as well-known for his work on
behalf of the Tibetan people as he is for his movie-star status.
Milton S. Hershey, although famous for his chocolate, gave
approximately $60 million to a school he founded for orphan
boys. Few people exemplify the meaning of service more than
Virgo Mother Teresa, whose work on behalf of the poor is legendary and earned her the Nobel Peace Prize in 1979.

The deepest meaning of service is experienced when it is
accompanied by a sense of "higher calling." This quality is
characterized by doing something because your heart tells you
to, whether it is for people, animals, or for a cause such as the
environment.

Because the concept of service is so central for Virgos, be
mindful of whether or not your service has a deep sense of
purpose for you. Sometimes Virgos will do something for
someone not because they want to but because they think

they should. They think that they have to help someone, even if they do not want to, in order to be a "good" person. This kind of service doesn't engage your heart. All Virgos have a calling. You will recognize your calling from the wonderful feeling you experience when you do it.

Bringing It All Together

You have an uncanny talent with whatever you are doing, for seeing how all of the pieces fit together like a gigantic jigsaw puzzle. You know how to investigate, classify, and organize anything you put your mind to. Virgo Dr. Walter Reed conducted a series of experiments to see how diseases were transmitted. His research helped to prevent the spread of the typhoid and yellow fevers. Virgo Lee De Forest was an inventor at the age of thirteen and eventually held more than three hundred patents on radio and other electronic devices. He invented the Audion tube, which enabled the broadcasting of sound through radio.

In anything you do, whether editing the school paper, planning a community event, or investigating college possibilities, you are able to see all of the parts that must be considered. As with a jigsaw puzzle, placing each piece in its proper location reveals the whole picture. To be successful, keep your attention on the bigger picture as you carry out the steps to reach your goal.

Your Soul Mission: Distinguishing the Difference between High Standards and Perfectionism

What is perfection? This question is part of every Virgo's path. Because of your idealistic nature, it is natural for you to seek perfection in all that you do. But, what constitutes perfection is tricky because as you reach one goal there is always farther to go, another dream to fulfill.

When you look at a photograph, you can dissect it, noticing everything that is right or wrong. When you watch a movie, you know that something came before a particular scene and that something will come after. Although you make observations, you withhold judgment until the end. Your life, and everybody else's, is like a movie. Although it can be helpful to look at a particular picture or scene to analyze it, once that analysis is done, it needs to be placed back into the larger context. Life is a process. Make sure you do not focus on just one scene.

It is easy to find Virgos who are critical of themselves and hard on others. You get an image in your mind of how you or someone "should be." Wanting to improve or make something better is a wonderful quality. But, for Virgos, this desire can too easily turn into the habit of criticizing—of noticing what is wrong instead of what is right. Your high standards, when they are positive, affirming, and supportive, give you something to aim for, to make yours and others' lives better and more fulfilling. When your high standards turn into perfectionism, you will notice the accompanying feelings of anxiety and worry. Too often, when Virgos wait for perfection, they become observers of life instead of participants. Since the path toward achievement consists of making mistakes, count on making some! Your mistakes will inform you about what to do, or not to do again.

FRIENDSHIP

Mercury, the planet of the mind and communication, is your ruling planet. It makes conversation and shared interests or hobbies important in your friendships. By getting involved in activities such as working on the school paper or joining a book club, you are likely to make new friends. Because of your desire to help, organizations such as the Sierra Club, the Audubon Society, Habitat for Humanity, or programs that feed the homeless are also areas where you will meet like-minded people. For you, people with whom you form friendships do not necessarily have to be the same age. What is more important is that you have shared interests.

Your sweet and affectionate nature will help you make friends easily. You like being helpful to those you care about, and your friends appreciate this quality. You are not one who insists on getting your own way all of the time. However, make sure you let your friends be helpful to you also. You may be so busy making sure your friends are comfortable that you don't think enough about your own needs.

In friendships, as in all of your relationships, you like to take your time getting to know someone. Once you know someone, you like to stay friends for a long time. Your friends are important to you, and you enjoy creating long-lasting bonds.

Check out the compatibility guide later in this chapter to see how your friends' Sun signs match up with yours.

HOME LIFE

It is not as if there has never been a rebellious Virgo. But if Virgos rebel, it is because of something specific rather than just to be contrary. Virgos are rarely the troublemakers in a family. Instead, you are more likely to be helpful to your parents. In fact, you may focus on trying to be the "perfect" kid and not want to cause any problems. Or, you may worry about trying to meet the expectations of your parents. Sometimes the parents of Virgos give them more than they can handle. Since they don't hear complaints, they assume everything must be fine. It would be helpful for your parents to realize that you want to do everything right and are concerned about not failing the people you love. Make sure you do not set impossible expectations for yourself, because doing so could lead you to feel inadequate or to think that there is something wrong with you if you do not attain those high expectations.

It is important for you to have your own space in your bedroom where you can organize your belongings. Chaos in general can feel particularly uncomfortable for you. You are more likely to want everything in its proper place. Because of your strong mind, you probably want your books close by, along with the arts and crafts or other projects with which you are always busy. You are likely to be modest, so you need a fair amount of privacy. If it is not feasible to have your own bedroom, you at least need to have your own personal space whenever possible.

CAREER

The first requirement for a career choice is to be in touch with your ideals and then look at the practical steps you need to take to reach your goal. There is little you cannot do, so aim high!

You like to be busy, productive, and useful, so a job where there is little to do is definitely not for you. You are not looking to skate by in life, but instead want your abilities and talents to be used. Virgos have a great reputation as the sign with a good work ethic. Talk-show and game-show host Regis Philbin is a good example of a Virgo who worked hard in his business for many years and now enjoys the success that his efforts have produced.

Because you have a sincere desire to help others, you may be attracted to the helping professions, which include medicine, psychology, massage therapy, social work, or teaching. The health field in general is appealing to many Virgos. There are many Virgo nutritionists, fitness experts, acupuncturists, physical therapists, and other professionals who are involved with health and healing.

Any job that requires precision or attention to detail and uses your highly observant and discriminating talents could be very satisfying. Examples include a movie or restaurant critic, a fashion or design consultant, an editor, or an auto mechanic. Any job that requires skill in troubleshooting would not only be enjoyable, but also one in which you would excel.

Writing, acting, and music as well as other creative professions are attractive to Virgos. Actors Marlee Matlin, Jada

Pinkett Smith, Tommy Lee Jones, and Eric Stolz are a few. Some Virgo actors are also known for their comedic talents, including Bill Murray, Lily Tomlin, Adam Sandler, and Jane Curtin. Virgo songwriters and musicians include jazz great Charlie Parker, Elvis Costello, LeAnn Rimes, Shania Twain, Gloria Estefan, and Van Morrison. Some great Virgo authors are Richard Wright, Leo Tolstoy, and Upton Sinclair.

RELATIONSHIPS

Perfect Love

Virgos are discerning in their approach to relationships. You are not interested in superficial relationships and are not likely to waste your time dating people just to be going out with someone. You would much rather sit home and read a book than spend time with people whose company you do not enjoy.

Cautious in matters of love, you are willing to take your time getting to know someone to make sure a relationship feels right for you. But, paradoxically, because you are so idealistic, once you fall in love you have a tendency to throw that innate caution to the wind!

You have a great respect for the intellect, and you prefer someone who is communicative. You love holding hands while going for walks in nature and talking about your shared interests and those topics that matter the most to you. Meeting at a bookstore for quiet conversation or walking home from school together gives you the opportunity to get to know someone without the distraction of being around other people. You seek simplicity rather than drama in your relationships.

However, although you need someone you can talk with, talking too much will not do, either. After all, you are an earth sign! For you, love is demonstrated tangibly. Someone who helps and supports you as much as you are there for him or her really counts. All of the words in the world do not make up for someone who is not generous, kind, and ready to lend a hand. Love is demonstrated by doing things for each other.

Because you are generous, helpful, and supportive, you may find yourself attracted to people who could use your help. Make sure that you make your own needs important also. Do not put so much focus on making your loved one's life easier that you make your life harder.

Wonderfully idealistic when you fall in love, you start out seeing perfection in your loved one, while the naturally human imperfections show up later. When they do, it will be important for you to make some decisions about what you can live with. Your exceptional capacity for observation means you will notice things that many others do not even see. This can be a little unnerving for the person on whom you are focused! Some Virgos may be disappointed when human flaws appear; others will be practical about the short-comings of their loved one.

For many Virgos, there is a desire to help the other person improve. You will need to use great tact and sensitivity when discussing your needs and the other person's behavior. Being true to yourself is so important—but allowing room for people's faults is also essential in any relationship. Ultimately, the consideration you give to others mirrors the allowances you make for yourself.

Sign Compatibility

There are some basic concepts to keep in mind when you are thinking about compatibility. You want to remember that although Sun sign characteristics describe central and impor-tant themes in life, the Sun does not represent the *whole* per-son. Planets, particularly Venus, are also important to consider when determining compatibility between people. Venus is the planet that symbolizes your concept of an ideal relationship. It describes how you like to give and receive affection. The sign that Venus occupied at the time of your birth explains what is most important to you when you are in love. Other planets are equally important when it comes to relationships: Mercury is the planet that reveals your communication style; Mars is the planet of action and desire. The Moon shows your emotional temperament and security concerns.

Signs that are opposite each other in the zodiac are often compatible, although their personality characteristics are very different. Pisces is Virgo's opposite sign.

Now, with these considerations in place, we can proceed!

COMPATIBILITY GUIDE

Virgo and Aries
Both of you like to be active. An Aries does not tend to think things through, preferring spontaneity, while you are more grounded and like to plan your activities. Your Aries is attracted to your earthy sensibility, while you are intrigued by the Aries jump-out-and-do-it style.

The challenge: Although you are both idealistic and like to aim high, you have significantly different approaches to achieving your goals in life. You will need to make adjustments to each other's personal styles for this relationship to work.

Virgo and Taurus
This is a harmonious combination. Because you share the earth element, there is a level of comfort and ease in relating to each other. You love your Taurus's loyalty and affectionate nature. Your Taurus understands your needs and desires. You both are looking for a lasting commitment.

The challenge: Whereas you love simplicity, your Taurus loves luxury. You love to be active; a Taurus enjoys sitting still. Plan activities to do together to bring you closer to each other.

Virgo and Gemini
You share the same ruling planet, Mercury, which creates a special bond and understanding. When you are together, there is nothing the two of you can't discuss. You love your

Gemini's clever mind and playful personality, while he or she is attracted to your earthy sensibility.

The challenge: Although you are both thinkers, you tend to be more analytical and practical than a Gemini. Make allowances for the differences to help this relationship thrive.

Virgo and Cancer

This relationship is likely to feel comfortable from the very beginning. You are both innately cautious and are content to take your time getting to know each other. Supporting each other comes easily. This relationship can go as deep as you want it to go.

The challenge: Because neither of you really likes to rock the boat, you will have to make sure you discuss any problems that arise to keep this relationship on stable ground.

Virgo and Leo

Although you two have different temperaments, in many ways those differences can create compatibility. You are practical, while a Leo approaches life with a sense of drama. You love to help and Leos like to lead. Your Leo's generosity and your giving nature can make this relationship work.

The challenge: This relationship can get out of balance if you find you are doing too much of the work of the relationship. Make sure you let your Leo know what is important for you to keep this relationship strong.

Virgo and Virgo

The two of you totally understand each other. There are no mysteries or guessing games. Supporting and helping each other comes easily. You enjoy the same activities and sharing your deepest dreams. This relationship can feel magical from the beginning.

The challenge: Because you are both focused on improvement, make sure you do not get overly critical of each other to stay content in this relationship.

Virgo and Libra

You both are idealistic and appreciate someone with a good mind. You love the sociability and charm of your Libra, while your Libra is attracted to your affectionate and giving nature. Both of you love to spend time doing special things for each other.

The challenge: Neither of you is especially comfortable with conflict. You will need to make sure that you don't sweep problems under the rug to keep this relationship strong.

Virgo and Scorpio

There is nothing lazy in either of you. You respect each other's drive and intensity and enjoy the same kinds of activities. You are attracted to your Scorpio's strength, charisma, and charm. Your Scorpio loves your earthy, serious nature.

The challenge: Because you both tend to be serious, make a point to do fun activities to bring balance to your relationship.

Virgo and Sagittarius

With your high standards and expectations in life and your Sagittarius's big dreams, there is little the two of you cannot do. You both share an idealistic nature and are ready to make your mark on the world. Your Sagittarius's optimistic nature is a perfect counterbalance to your more down-to-earth personality.

The challenge: A Sagittarius needs lots of freedom and lacks the practicality that you have in abundance. To remain content, you will have to make sure that you do not spend too much time "cleaning up" after your Sagittarius.

Virgo and Capricorn

Both earth signs, you instinctively understand each other. You share a commonsense approach to life and have similar interests. Your Capricorn supports your goals and understands your dreams. There is little you will not do to be there for each other.

The challenge: Since both of you are serious and hard-working, make sure you take time to play to keep this relationship balanced.

Virgo and Aquarius

Both of you have high standards, although your definitions of them may be a bit different. You both appreciate a strong mind and find plenty to talk about. You are intrigued by your Aquarius's independent nature. Your Aquarius appreciates your grounded approach to life. Life is always interesting when you two are together!

The challenge: Although you love your Aquarius's independent nature, since you tend to be more cautious, you will both need to accommodate these differences in your personalities for this relationship to stay on track.

Virgo and Pisces

Pisces is your opposite sign, which forms a natural attraction. You are both idealistic, although you are much more practical. You love your Pisces' imaginative, dreamy nature, while your Pisces is attracted to your can-do personality. You both are compassionate people and love to do things for each other.

The challenge: As with all opposite signs, your strengths and weaknesses are also opposite. Your Pisces is stronger in the feeling and faith department, while you have a more commonsense approach to the world. Learning from each other brings balance into this relationship.

SPECIAL TIPS FOR VIRGOS

Below are reminders and special tips that will help any Virgo lead a successful and fulfilling life. Maximize your positive traits, and be aware of those traits that can hold you back. Make the effort to learn from your mistakes, and keep your eyes on the stars!

1. Have faith in your abilities; pursue your dreams.
2. Balance practicality and idealism.
3. Take time to play.
4. Do not let observations turn into judgments.
5. Don't do something just to keep busy. Make sure your heart and soul are in it.
6. See perfection in imperfection.
7. Take risks. Participate in life.
8. When you help people, make sure you are serving, rather than being subservient.
9. Don't be hard on yourself; don't be hard on others.
10. Be helpful rather than critical.

✳

You, dear Virgo, with your wonderful combination of practicality and idealism, can succeed in any area you apply your exceptional mind. Your high standards are an advantage. They will help you fulfill your greatest dreams. With your talents, you can accomplish anything you desire.

✳

Libra

The Peacemaker

September 23 to October 23

Symbol: The Scales
Ruling planet: Venus
Element: Air—*social, communicative, detached*
Mode: Cardinal—*energetic, initiating, active*
Birthstone: Opal
Color: Green

FAMOUS LIBRA PEOPLE:

September 23	Ani DiFranco	September 28	Gwyneth
September 24	Linda		Paltrow
	McCartney	September 29	Lech Walesa
September 25	Will Smith	September 30	Jenna Elfman
September 26	Serena	October 1	Annie Besant
	Williams	October 2	Mahatma
September 27	Arthur Penn		Gandhi

October 3	Neve Campbell	October 14	e. e. cummings
October 4	Anne Rice	October 15	Sarah Ferguson
October 5	Kate Winslet	October 16	Tim Robbins
October 6	Jenny Lind	October 17	Margot Kidder
October 7	Toni Braxton	October 18	Jean-Claude Van
October 8	Matt Damon		Damme
October 9	John Lennon	October 19	John Lithgow
October 10	Ben Vereen	October 20	Arthur Rimbaud
October 11	Eleanor Roosevelt	October 21	Ursula Le Guin
October 12	Marion Jones	October 22	Deepak Chopra
October 13	Kelly Preston	October 23	Johnny Carson

THESE BEHAVIORS AND ATTITUDES
INCREASE CONFIDENCE

Fairness
Cooperation
Sociability
Diplomacy
Idealism
Friendliness
Considerateness

THESE BEHAVIORS AND ATTITUDES
DECREASE CONFIDENCE

Avoidance
Indecision
Evasiveness
Insincerity
Dependency
Fantasizing
Inauthenticity

THE PEACEMAKER

You, dear Libra, are the peacemaker. Your presence makes this world a more harmonious and beautiful place. Like your symbol, the scales, you love to keep everything in balance. Nothing distresses you more than when people argue and are mean to one another. A Libra enters life knowing something that many other people spend a lifetime learning—that there are people in this world besides you! You know this truth coming out of the womb. It seems so simple to you. You excel at finding areas where you can agree with others and are content to take your differences and put them into perspective. You seek common ground and are convinced that if people could discuss their differences calmly, this world would be a better place.

There are numerous Libra peacemakers in the world. Former president of the United States Jimmy Carter continues to play a major role in the world by mediating international disputes. He travels to the world's most difficult places to help people find peaceful solutions to problems, conflicts, and differences in their countries. Jesse Jackson did what no one else was able to do when he secured the release of hostages in both Libya and Kosovo. Lech Walesa founded the labor union Solidarity, which helped end communism in Poland and led the way to democratic elections. He eventually became a president of Poland. Poet and writer Václav Havel helped to lead his country, the Czech Republic, to democracy and was elected its president in 1993. Archbishop Desmond Tutu joined with Nelson Mandela to bring justice to South Africa by leading the Truth and Reconciliation Commission. Mahatma Gandhi utilized the powerful and spiritual form of nonviolent resistance to bring an end to British rule and bring self-rule to India. Look for an area in the world that has been transformed into a more harmonious and beautiful place and you will find a Libra who convinced others that a better world was possible.

Your natural gift of diplomacy allows you to take something that is hard for someone to hear and make it sound like the most wonderful thing in the world! You are a born mediator. You are so respectful of other people that you can convince almost anybody into coming halfway. Compromise is fine with you. You are a realist when it comes to knowing that we live in a world with a variety of views. You are less interested in changing people's minds than in helping people with different beliefs to get along. People seek you out because they know that you will listen to them and that they will get a fair hearing.

Manifesting Your Dream

Idealism is one of a Libra's most wonderful traits. Your idealism prompts you to make the world a fairer, more just, more loving, and more beautiful place. Libra musician Bob Geldof idealistically thought that he could convince other musicians to donate their time and talent to a rock-concert benefit to help starving people in Africa. Through that concert, Live Aid, he raised $70 million. This incredible event launched the trend of musicians speaking out and performing benefits for a variety of social and humanitarian causes. Eleanor Roosevelt (the wife of president Franklin D. Roosevelt) devoted herself to a variety of humanitarian causes during her twelve years as First Lady. Later, as a delegate to the United Nations and as chairperson of the UN Commission on Human Rights, she was instrumental in the adoption of the Universal Declaration of Human Rights. In the seventeenth century, when England's King Charles II granted Quaker William Penn the province of Pennsylvania, Penn's idealism encouraged him to sign friendship treaties with the local Native Americans so that the colonists and they could live in peace with one another.

Because Libras are so charming and diplomatic, some people mistake them for shrinking violets. Nothing could be further from the truth. You love to take the initiative. It is this combination of idealism and initiative that allows you to accomplish great things. The late Linda McCartney, Beatle

Paul McCartney's wife, was an impressive crusader for animal rights. She even created her own frozen–vegetarian food business.

It is important for your idealism to have a focus, to have a place for expression. Otherwise dreams too easily stay in the fantasy stage, where you think about how great something could be without doing anything to bring about what you want.

What do you want to do? Where do your ideals lead you? Allow your visions for your future to motivate you to manifest your dreams.

It's Okay with Me If It's Okay with You

You may have been told you are indecisive. Libras can have a hard time making up their minds—not because they are unable to, but because they are highly aware that all points of view and all choices have merit. If someone asks you if you think a friend made a poor or good decision about something, you would probably weigh the pros and cons and be able to justify the validity of whatever choice was made. When someone offers you an option such as "Would you rather go to the movies or to the mall?" you may ask what he or she would prefer. The fact is you like to know the other person is content with the chosen activity. And, often you really do not mind which activity is chosen. People have a hard time understanding Libras in this regard. Many people are so used to making sure that they get their own way that it can be hard for them to understand someone who does not always have a preference. However, since you sometimes have trouble speaking up for yourself, take the time to determine if your lack of preference is because you really do not care or because you are afraid you will upset someone by stating your needs or desires.

Your Soul Mission: Balancing the Scales

Because Libras dislike conflict, you may not speak up for yourself when it is important for you to do so. You may think that it is not worth the trouble to let people know when you disagree with them or when you do not appreciate the way someone is treating you. You may think fairness constitutes making excuses for the bad behavior of others. Or, you may think that expressing your own needs or speaking up for yourself is selfish. It is important for you to feel secure in your highly developed sense of fairness. You are not going to become a selfish, egotistical person if you speak up for yourself! It is important for you to know that your needs and feelings are just as important as those of someone else.

Libras need to make sure they speak up. Hiding behind that beautiful smile of yours, you can be quite upset without anyone's knowing it. If you don't let people know what you are thinking and feeling, the time may come when you do not know, either. So eager to not rock the boat, you put energy into keeping a calm surface when a storm is brewing beneath. You cannot devalue your own needs and keep things in balance when the surface is calm but the depths are stormy.

Trust your natural sense of diplomacy and have confidence that you can cope with a little conflict in your relationships. You have such a beautiful way of speaking and explaining concepts that you can bring this talent into the more personal areas of your life. The valuable quality of assertiveness provides a perfect balance to your naturally considerate personality. Remember, Lech Walesa could not have helped to change his country for the better if he had not upset a few people. Use the warrior spirit that is so easy for you to access when it comes to the rights of others, and use it to stand up for your own rights.

Fairness is your motto. It is a word you use often and a concept that is close to your heart. Your challenge in life is to make sure that while you are fair to others, you are also fair to yourself. Keeping those Libra scales balanced means including yourself! Otherwise the scales are tipped with the other person being all the way at the top while you are all the way at the bottom. This is not balance—even if no one is making a fuss or having an argument. Part of what you are learning in life is that fairness and cooperation does not mean making your own needs unimportant.

FRIENDSHIP

Libras are kind and considerate friends. Genuinely interested in their lives and concerns, you can attract friends like bees to honey. You have a special gift for giving people the kind of attention and affection that makes them feel like the only person in the world. Many people count you as one of their best friends. You probably do best hanging out with one friend at a time rather than in a group of them. You simply excel at and love the one-on-one interaction.

Make sure you stay in touch with your own needs within your friendships. Do not keep inside things that need to be talked about. A Libra's tendency to avoid disagreements may prevent you from being true to yourself. Your natural communication skills and diplomacy will help you handle any problems that need to be discussed. You know how to support your friends. Make sure that you give them a chance to support you, too!

Because you are a lover of peace and justice, you are likely to make plenty of friends through organizations that help others. In fact, this is a wonderful way for you to meet new people with common interests.

Check out the compatibility guide later in this chapter to see how your friends' Sun signs match up with yours.

HOME LIFE

Libras are generally not the children in the family who throw tantrums to get what they want. In fact, you are more likely to be the one whom other family members choose to discuss their problems with. As a peacemaker, it is particularly hard on you when members of your family argue, and you will do everything you can to help them get along. This is your environment for learning how to be a great mediator. Your siblings may seek you out, knowing that they will get a fair hearing from you. Your parents may want you to be on their side during an argument. It is easy for you to end up in the middle.

Libras do not want to add to any conflict in the family. You want to stay out of trouble. If trying to keep the peace doesn't work, you may opt to spend extra time in school or participating in extracurricular activities.

Some Libras come from families who place a strong emphasis on the values of fairness and justice. Family members may be involved in professions or causes that seek to help others.

Because it is important for you to experience harmony in your environment, make sure that your bedroom—or, if you share your bedroom, the area around your bed—feels peaceful to you. Surround yourself with beautiful things, whether that be a poster of a beautiful scene or fancy cars, a bedspread in a color that you love, or some flowers in a colorful vase. For a Libra, creating a beautiful environment contributes to a sense of peace and harmony within.

CAREER

The overall environment at work should be harmonious. Since it is upsetting to you when people do not get along, you will do everything in your power to create a peaceful atmosphere. Coworkers are likely to appreciate and benefit from your efforts.

Although many Libras end up in positions of authority, it requires work to develop the necessary confidence in order to take the leadership reins. Leading others is easier when you feel your inner authority and are willing to risk disagreement.

You are a people person who enjoys communicating and socializing, so careers that provide plenty of contact with others are natural choices for you. Becoming a psychologist, an astrologer, or a counselor of any kind may interest you. Selling real estate, products, or ideas are also avenues for you to explore. Careers where establishing a relationship with others is essential utilizes your natural gifts.

The world is full of Libra lawyers and judges, both of which professions require being able to consider another person's point of view. Work in mediation, conflict resolution, or arbitration would come easily to you.

With your natural love of beauty and your artistic nature, all professions that require a developed sense of beauty, harmony, and design are tailor-made for you. Some examples of this are interior or landscape design, architecture, painting, or anything in the beauty professions, such as a fashion designer, makeup artist, or hairstylist. Your sociability lends itself to any career where entertaining people and helping them to have a good time is important. Some examples are jobs in the hotel, restaurant, or catering businesses, or a job producing parties and events.

Because the concepts of fairness and justice are so close to your heart, working for organizations that promote these concepts and ideals are perfect, whether it is Amnesty International, Doctors Without Borders, or an organization that helps animals.

RELATIONSHIPS

Love Makes the World Go Around

With Venus (which is named after the Roman goddess of love) as your ruling planet, you are quite romantic and like all of the rituals of getting to know another. You adore gallant, dramatic gestures and grand declarations of love. If someone would lay his or her coat over a puddle for you or walk several miles just to visit with you for a few minutes, you would positively swoon and pledge your everlasting love. You are attracted to knights in shining armor or heroic maidens such as Joan of Arc, who led troops into battle for a just and worthy cause.

You have a great attitude toward a relationship. You give it your all. You encourage the person you care for to express his or her needs and desires. You are the best cheerleader anyone could ever have. Eager to shower your affection on someone, you absolutely glow when you have someone with whom to share yourself.

Because you dislike conflict, you may let your sweetie get away with a little too much. Make sure you do not love being in a relationship so much that you lose your own sense of individuality. Giving 100 percent to a relationship is healthy and natural for you, which is different from *giving yourself over to* a relationship. Make sure you are not obtaining your sense of self from the other person. Otherwise if that person leaves, your sense of self will leave also.

The writer Antoine de Saint Exupéry wrote, "Love does not consist in gazing at each other but in looking together in the same direction." Self-love is an essential ingredient in any relationship. Affirm every day the wonderful, lovable, and unique qualities that make you so special. Make sure that you are happy with who *you* are.

Libras are often attracted to someone who has some rough edges and who could use some of their gentle peacemaker energy. Adventurous, assertive people are really attractive to you. You love confident types who know exactly what they are doing and where they are going. They are a great complement to your see-all-points-of-view personality. You welcome someone who takes charge.

However, sometimes a dragon slayer turns into the dragon! Those assertive, I-know-what-I-want types may end up being so concerned with what *they* want that after the courtship phase is over, they stop paying attention to what *you* want. Make sure that the self-assured person is just that—and not a selfish have-to-have-my-own-way type.

Sign Compatibility

There are some basic concepts to keep in mind when you are thinking about compatibility. You want to remember that although Sun sign characteristics describe central and important themes in life, the Sun does not represent the *whole* person. Planets, particularly Venus, are also important to consider when determining compatibility between people. Venus is the planet that symbolizes your concept of an ideal relationship. It describes how you like to give and receive affection. The sign that Venus occupied at the time of your birth explains what is most important to you when you are in love. Other planets are equally important when it comes to relationships: Mercury is the planet that reveals your communication style; Mars is the planet of action and desire. The Moon shows your emotional temperament and security concerns.

Signs that are opposite each other in the zodiac are often compatible, although their personality characteristics are very different. Aries is Libra's opposite sign.

Now, with these considerations in place, we can proceed!

COMPATIBILITY GUIDE

Libra and Aries

Libra and Aries are opposite signs and have opposite approaches to life. You love the confidence, the gutsy quality, and the courage of an Aries as much as an Aries loves your charm, grace, and sociability. You are both idealistic and enjoy making your dreams come true with each other.

The challenge: Since an Aries is quite independent and likes to be on the move, make sure you give your Aries plenty of room to help this relationship thrive.

Libra and Taurus

Taurus shares your ruling planet, Venus, the planet of love, so the connection between you is strong. You love your Taurus's loyalty and strength. Your Taurus is attracted to your romantic nature. Whether talking or spending quiet time together, it is easy for you two to feel close.

The challenge: As an air sign, you tend to be more social and communicative than a Taurus. You will need to make some adjustments to each other's personal styles for this relationship to gel.

Libra and Gemini

The two of you can spend hours talking to each other. Because both of you are air signs, communication is important and an easy way for you to connect. You love the cleverness of your Gemini's mind, and your Gemini appreciates how smart and tuned in you are.

The challenge: Although you are both strong communicators, you may not share your feelings on more difficult personal topics. Make sure you keep all lines of communication open for this relationship to last.

Libra and Cancer

You adore your Cancer's compassion and sensitivity. Your Cancer loves your desire to be connected and close. Neither of you likes to make a fuss and instead you both prefer to focus on ways of remaining close to each other. Although you come from different elements, you are both seeking a heart connection.

The challenge: Both of you are likely to avoid conflict, which can prevent you from discussing important matters concerning your relationship. You will need to find a way to talk about your problems for this relationship to work.

Libra and Leo

You both share a creative and artistic nature and are both romantics at heart. You adore your Leo's strength and confidence. Your Leo is enchanted by your grace and charm. When you express your love and admiration for a Leo, there is nothing he or she will not do for you.

The challenge: Because Leos are so strong, it may be difficult for you to assert your needs when it is important for you to do so. Considering your own desires as well as your Leo's keeps this relationship balanced.

Libra and Virgo

You love the down-to-earth, unpretentious nature of your Virgo. Your Virgo adores your love of togetherness. You are both idealistic and have high standards. Because you both appreciate someone with a good mind, intellectual discussions are extra-enjoyable.

The challenge: Your Virgo is much more practical than you are and keeps track of things you do not even notice. Appreciate your Virgo's earthy sensibilities to help this relationship thrive.

Libra and Libra

There are many Libra couples in this world. You are both natural romantics and nothing feels easier than being together. You both love a great discussion and excel at listening to, understanding, and supporting each other's dreams and goals.

The challenge: Because both of you are uncomfortable with conflict, make sure that you speak your mind when it is important to do so. Otherwise tension will build because of too many unresolved issues.

Libra and Scorpio

You both are looking for a deep, soul connection with each other. You love the magnetic charisma of your Scorpio and the fact that your Scorpio will go to the ends of the earth and back for you. You easily share your deepest thoughts and dreams with each other.

The challenge: You are more social and communicative than your Scorpio, who likes to spend a fair amount of time alone. Since your Scorpio is from the water element, be sensitive to his or her feelings for this relationship to become strong.

Libra and Sagittarius

Life is an adventure when you are with a Sagittarius. Your Sagittarius has a great sense of humor and is fun to be with. You capture a Sagittarius's heart by your charming personality. Life is a bit of a roller coaster with your Sagittarius and worth every minute of the ride!

The challenge: You prefer spending more time together than your Sagittarius, who needs lots of freedom. Give your Sagittarius the space he or she needs to help this relationship along.

Libra and Capricorn

Your Capricorn is earthy and ambitious. You love people who know where they are going and how to get there. Your Capricorn takes love seriously and likes planning for the future. You are both dreamers at heart and love dreaming together.

The challenge: Capricorns are often more tenderhearted than they appear. Be sensitive to your Capricorn's feelings, while also making sure you discuss your own to help this relationship to flourish.

Libra and Aquarius

With an Aquarius you will never be at a loss for something to talk about. You both share the air element and love to discuss issues and plans for the future. Aquarians are truly unique, and you admire their originality and independent spirit. When you are with an Aquarius, life is fun, unpredictable, and exciting!

The challenge: Aquarians love to spend time with their friends. Become a part of the group to make this relationship work!

Libra and Pisces

You are both natural-born romantics and know how to tune into each other's mind, heart, and soul. You are often psychic with each other and may not need words to communicate. Both of you are naturally artistic, imaginative, and creative and have a wonderful time manifesting your dreams with each other.

The challenge: You are more of a communicator than your Pisces. You will need to give your Pisces quiet time for this relationship to grow.

SPECIAL TIPS FOR LIBRAS

Here are some reminders and special tips that will help any
Libra lead a successful and fulfilling life. Maximize your positive traits, and be aware of those traits that can hold you
back. Make the effort to learn from your mistakes, and keep
your eyes on the stars!

1. Be fair to yourself.
2. Do not let anyone convince you to be less idealistic.
3. Love yourself so that your sense of worth does not come
   from somebody else.
4. It is perfectly fine to say no.
5. Do not pretend that things are okay when they are not.
   Find somebody you can talk to.
6. Keep the scales balanced.
7. Take the risk to communicate with people openly and
   honestly.
8. Appreciate your desire to be cooperative.
9. It is important for you to be true to yourself even if somebody else does not agree with you.
10. Give the world the gift of your peacemaker energy.

✳

You, dear Libra, are a peacemaker. Your idealism, your
highly developed sense of fairness, your attunement to
beauty, and your considerate nature will take you very far in
life. When you use these extraordinary gifts, there is nothing
that you cannot accomplish.

✳

Scorpio

The Influencer

October 23 to November 22

Symbols: The Scorpion, the Eagle, and the Phoenix
Ruling planet: Pluto
Element: Water—*sensitive, intuitive, deep feelings*
Mode: Fixed—*determined, loyal, stubborn*
Birthstone: Topaz
Colors: Red and black

FAMOUS SCORPIO PEOPLE:

October 23	Michael Crichton	October 30	Christopher Columbus
October 24	Kevin Kline	October 31	Michael Landon
October 25	Pablo Picasso	November 1	Lyle Lovett
October 26	Natalie Merchant	November 2	k. d. lang
October 27	John Cleese	November 3	Dennis Miller
October 28	Bill Gates	November 4	Matthew McConaughey
October 29	Winona Ryder		

November 5	Tatum O'Neal	November 13	Whoopi Goldberg
November 6	Ethan Hawke	November 14	Claude Monet
November 7	Joni Mitchell	November 15	Georgia O'Keeffe
November 8	Bonnie Raitt	November 16	Lisa Bonet
November 9	Dorothy Dandridge	November 17	Martin Scorsese
		November 18	Alan Shepard
November 10	John P. Marquand	November 19	Jodie Foster
November 11	Leonardo DiCaprio	November 20	Nadine Gordimer
November 12	Elizabeth Cady Stanton	November 21	Goldie Hawn
		November 22	Jamie Lee Curtis

THESE BEHAVIORS AND ATTITUDES INCREASE CONFIDENCE

Resourcefulness
Determination
Effectiveness
Magnetism
Sensitivity
Charisma
Intuition
Strong will

THESE BEHAVIORS AND ATTITUDES DECREASE CONFIDENCE

Manipulation
Controlling tendency
Secretiveness
Coldness
Vengefulness
Obsessiveness
Inflexibility
Suspicion

THE INFLUENCER

You, dear Scorpio, have the extraordinary destiny of being an influencer. You have the ability to affect others by your strength, determination, and charisma. The word *influence* comes from a term meaning "to flow." Interestingly, one of the definitions for *influence* from *Merriam-Webster's Collegiate Dictionary,* 10th ed., is: "an ethereal fluid held to flow from the stars and to affect the actions of humans." This ability to influence means you have the gift of working closely with power. The decisions you make about what kind of influence you want to be and what kind of affect you want to have on people and the world are part of every Scorpio's path.

The world has given us plenty of Scorpios who have wielded great influence. Scorpio Bill Gates, computer genius and cofounder of the Microsoft Corporation, has been a pivotal force in the computer industry and in the world of technology. Ted Turner revolutionized the reporting of world news when he introduced twenty-four-hour live news broadcasts through his cable television network CNN. He is now influencing how the world helps countries in need through his $1 billion gift to the United Nations. Elizabeth Cady Stanton was a significant figure in the struggle for women's rights. Her work contributed to the passage of the Nineteenth Amendment, which gave women the right to vote.

What all of these people have in common is their incredible determination, foresight, and ability to influence the tide of history. Clearly, as a Scorpio you can do just about anything you put your mind to.

Determined to Succeed

Scorpio is a fixed sign, which means you are blessed with tremendous determination. No one has ever accused you of being easygoing or laid-back! There is little you cannot achieve if you set your mind to it because when you make up your mind to do something, you give it your body, heart, and soul.

When nineteen-year-old Scorpio Gertrude Ederle, a triple-Olympic-gold-medal winner in swimming, was told to cancel her swim across the English Channel because of storms that had closed the channel to shipping, she answered, "What for?" She went on to swim across in record time and became the first woman to do so. Florence Sabin, an anatomist, led an exceptional life, becoming the first woman to be made a full professor at Johns Hopkins University in 1917, and in 1925 she was the first woman to be elected to the National Academy of Sciences. Christopher Columbus sailed across the ocean during a time when many thought the world was flat. Whoopi Goldberg overcame the obstacle of poverty to become a famous actress and comedienne. These Scorpios set out to accomplish something and let nothing stand in their way.

Make sure you are setting goals for yourself. Your energy needs a focus and a direction. You are able to overcome obstacles in your path once you have decided to achieve something. A bored, directionless Scorpio is an unhappy Scorpio! Don't waste your exceptional internal resources of drive and determination.

The Scorpion, the Eagle, and the Phoenix

Scorpio is such a powerful and somewhat complex sign that it has three symbols: the scorpion, the eagle, and the phoenix. The scorpion is associated with traits such as being selfish, mean, or vengeful and purposely seeking to make others feel bad or have troubles. The scorpion symbolizes self-destruction and the destruction of others. Conversely, the eagle flies above these lower impulses and has a greater view and more objectivity. The eagle's qualities are loyalty and support of others. The eagle is courageous and puts great energy into achieving its aims in the world. In the phoenix, a symbol of the cycle of death and rebirth, the eagle is transformed into a mythical bird that rises fully empowered from the ashes of the past. The phoenix is the result of transformation by life's experiences. Instead of being cynical and bitter, it understands that harmony and love can come after working through conflict and that dawn comes after the darkness of night. By allowing yourself to become transformed by your experiences, you not only become powerful, you become the phoenix. Most Scorpios have the experience of each of these three symbols at different times in their lives.

Swimming in Deep Waters

Scorpio is from the water element, the world of feelings. And, although you respond to the world through your emotions like the other two water signs (Cancer and Pisces), your sensitivity tends to be based on a kind of instinctual awareness, along with deep wisdom and psychic hunches. Many people who go into the business world are Scorpios who use this sensitivity—an ability to feel where things are and where they are headed.

Scorpios have a tendency to hold in their feelings, which can become harmful. It is important to talk about your feelings. Find someone with whom you can safely talk about what is going on inside of you, whether it is a family member, friend, school counselor, or a teacher. Holding in your feelings is like damming up a river so that it cannot flow freely. The power and majesty of a river is expressed when it flows with all its force.

The Importance of Privacy

Scorpio celebrities, for the most part, guard their privacy fiercely, giving few interviews. When you do finally hear from them, they do not talk much about their personal life and you still feel like you don't know much about who they are. Julia Roberts, Calista Flockhart, Jodie Foster, Ethan Hawke, Leonardo DiCaprio, Demi Moore, k. d. lang, and Natalie Merchant are a few of the many Scorpio entertainers who are known for protecting their privacy.

Honoring the need for privacy is important for Scorpios. Your inner world, your feelings, motivations, and thoughts should be revealed only when you feel comfortable doing so. Although part of a Scorpio's path is learning to become more comfortable sharing thoughts and feelings, it is also important to be private when you feel the need.

Because you do not reveal your feelings easily, sometimes people think you are cold. The fact is, as a water sign, you feel everything very deeply. But, because you are not comfortable showing everyone your feelings, people may see little of what is going on inside of you. Like a glacier in the ocean, only the tip is visible. Most of it is hidden beneath the surface. Your emotions, although strong and intense, also often lie just below the surface. Part of your life journey will be learning how to comfortably bring your feelings up for air. Allowing them to flow helps to channel your emotions and release your creativity.

Trust: Can I Count on You?

Being private or even secretive is related to the issue of trust. There is no question that there are untrustworthy people in this world. And Scorpios have a unique radar, an instinct that picks up on some of the least desirable characteristics in human nature. You get gut feelings about people and sometimes see something about them that they may not even know about themselves.

If someone has broken your trust, you may decide to trust no one. The problem with that decision is that you end up not trusting completely trustworthy people as well. Part of a Scorpio's job is learning to distinguish the difference. Ultimately, all trust issues are learning about self-trust, as in "Can I count on myself to know whom I can trust?" It is important for you to have someone you can rely on and talk to. If you do not have that right now, make it a top priority to cultivate a close, trusting relationship.

The Nature of Power

What is power? Power can be used to heal or to wound, to help people or to hurt them. Power in itself is neither good nor bad—it just is. The use of power is one of a Scorpio's most important themes. Because you are a person of influence, how you utilize your power is very important. You have seen people abuse their power. Have you seen people use their power to help others and therefore influence them positively? Perhaps a teacher or a relative has gone out of his or her way to help you or someone else. If a kid at school needs help and you decide to help him or her, you will have used your power positively. You have decided to be a good influence. If a friend of yours is making fun of someone and you join in, you have used your power negatively. It can be that simple. Power is about making choices.

Creating Options, Perceiving Choices

Feeling empowered is having the knowledge that there are infinite options and choices in any situation. Experiencing your power means holding on to it rather than giving it to someone else. Whenever you allow someone else to determine how you feel about yourself, you have given that person the power that belongs to you. Whenever you think that there is nothing you can do about a situation in which you find yourself, you have given away your power—literally your ability to act and to make choices. If you think in extremes, that there are only two choices, you have disempowered yourself. This is a common habit that Scorpios need to break. Thinking in extremes means you think in either/or terms, as in "Either I can do this, or I can do that." This gives you only two options, both of which may be unattractive.

Anytime you feel stuck or trapped and think you have no options or choices, think again and write a list of at least five options. You are not committing to any of them, you are simply writing them down to remember that you have options. Even if you still live with your parents and are not completely in charge of your life, you still have a variety of alternatives. After a while, thinking up options for all of the situations you encounter will become a natural habit. And, it will mean that you are totally in touch with your power.

Centering in Your Power

Because Scorpios are working with power issues, it is important for you to be in a position of power. It feels good to be in charge of something and makes use of your natural abilities. Become president of a club at school; get an after-school job so you can earn your own money; or play a sport that gives you the satisfaction of gaining control and mastery over your body. Many Scorpios gravitate toward the martial arts not only because it is about controlling your body, but also it helps bring together your body, mind, emotions, and spirit.

Whether or not you are completely in charge of your life, the fact is that you are completely in charge of your inner world. Nobody but you can decide how to think, feel, or act. This is where total empowerment resides for everybody. It is through your own choices and decisions that you will ultimately form and create your life. Here are some good things to ask yourself as you are faced with making choices every day: "Is this decision going to make me feel better or worse about myself?"; "Will I feel more confident or less confident?"; "Is this choice influencing my life in a good or bad way?"

The Power of the Mind

Your laserlike ability to focus is one of your gifts, which gives you a deep, probing, resourceful mind and the ability to stay with something no matter what. You have a phenomenal ability to concentrate for long periods of time. You are an excellent problem-solver. When people you know are in a crisis or having a hard time, you know just how to help them. This powerful mind and unique wisdom of yours will take you very far in life.

Many Scorpios excel at jobs having to do with research or investigation, since both require focus and persistence. But this quality can also cause you to obsess or worry about things in the world over which you have no control. Learning to channel your powerful mind in the direction that you want it to go is one of a Scorpio's challenges in life. Exercising your options will help you to do this.

Your Soul Mission: Learning When to Let Go and Move On

What should you do when things are not going the way you want them to go? Or, when people are not doing what you want them to do? One of the side effects of working with power is the impulse to control—and there is not a Scorpio alive who has not had to work intimately with this theme. The desire to control is anchored in the issue of trust—trust in people and trust in life. The impulse to control is caused by your desire to have someone you can count on, to have a world you can count on. But, both people and the world can be remarkably uncooperative.

Many Scorpios think that if people behave in a certain way or events go the way they want them to, happiness will result. But, that kind of happiness is fleeting because it is totally dependent upon others. True, lasting happiness is attained in exactly the opposite way. It is by letting go of trying to control people or outcomes that happiness and inner peace are found. This is the process of surrender that many philosophers and spiritual leaders speak about.

Learning to let go of trying to change anything other than yourself is a process, takes time, and is part of what being a Scorpio is all about. Your tremendous will, strength, and determination, when applied to yourself, activate your power. And, once your power is activated, you can do just about anything. There is nothing within yourself you cannot change.

When it is necessary to let go of a cherished desire, utilize your willpower and strength. Control where your thoughts go so you can perceive the variety of options that are available to you.

As for all water signs, cultivating the air element brings objectivity and clarity. Breathe deeply to help you gain distance from your feelings so that you can attain perspective. Seek input from an air sign (Gemini, Libra, or Aquarius).

FRIENDSHIP

For Scorpios, loyalty is an important ingredient in your friendships. You enjoy forming deep, long-lasting friendships and are likely to have many of the same friends now that you have known since childhood. You are generous and affectionate, and there is little you would not do for a friend. Since you are so good at problem-solving, when your friends have troubles, you excel at helping them figure out what to do.

It takes a while for you to get to know someone. You need to feel comfortable with a new friend before you open up and let that person know much about you. For you, trust comes with time. Although you may have a number of acquaintances, you are quite content to have one or two close friends who know you well. You need plenty of time alone, so you are not looking to overschedule yourself with a lot of activities.

Since you are more sensitive than you let on to others, people may unintentionally hurt your feelings and never even know it. Make sure you let your friends know what is going on with you. Another area of potential difficulty for you may be when a good friend also becomes friends with someone else. You treasure your close friends and enjoy spending time with them. Even though you love them to be available when you are, sharing your friends will feel easier over time.

If a friend betrays you, it may feel difficult to move on emotionally. Make sure you do not spend too much time nursing grudges or resentments. Instead, form new friendships with trustworthy people. Part of being a powerful person is knowing when to let go of the past.

Check out the compatibility guide later in this chapter to see how your friends' Sun signs match up with yours.

HOME LIFE

Because of your privacy needs, one of the most important factors in your home life is to have a place to go where you can be alone. When you spend the necessary time by yourself, you will be in a much better mood when you are around family members. Although you may not share your feelings with your parents, it is important to have someone you trust and with whom you can talk about the things that are important to you.

You are very much your own person and like to rely on yourself rather than the advice of others. You are likely to rebel against family rules. Nothing bothers you more than when your parents or other family members try to tell you what to do. Negotiate when you can. Since you need to feel some control over your life, this is an area where you may want to write down a list of options. List those things that are most important to you. Empower yourself within your family by seeking compromise. Since all relationships involve give-and-take, you will need to make sure you give a little to get a little.

It is preferable for you to have your own bedroom. If that is not feasible, try to create a space that is as private as possible. Many Scorpios prefer a dark bedroom, so thick curtains are a must! Blacks, browns, and deep reds are favorite Scorpio colors for decoration.

CAREER

Many Scorpios gravitate toward being in positions of authority and power. But, Scorpios who wield influence and are in positions of power are not just interested in being in charge. They have a passion about what they do, and it is their intensity, determination, and drive that is their fuel. Scorpio

Soichiro Honda had a passion for cars. He loved building race cars and manufacturing engines. He ultimately had more than one hundred patents and formed the Honda Motor Company. Bill Gates glows when he talks about his company, Microsoft. Film director Martin Scorsese's intensity and enthusiasm are evident when he speaks about his films. You get the idea that these people would still do the same job whether or not they were paid.

For you, too, it is important to pursue your passion. When the time comes to choose a career, your feelings will guide you in the right direction. Trust your intuition and in your ability to fulfill your dreams and to direct your life.

Because Scorpios are very interested in probing the mysteries of life and investigating the unknown, there are many Scorpio psychologists, researchers, doctors, nurses, and healers of all kinds. Scorpio Marie Curie received two Nobel Prizes, one in physics, for the discovery of radioactivity, and the other in chemistry, for isolating pure radium. Christiaan Barnard, a surgeon, performed the first human-heart transplant. Jonas Edward Salk created the polio vaccine. Scorpios' love of mystery attracts them to police work to solve crimes, to writing mystery novels, or even to exploring the mysteries of space. John P. Marquand won a Pulitzer Prize for his detective stories. Alan Shepard was the first American in space. Carl Sagan devoted his life to exploring the mysteries of the universe. British astronomer Edmund Halley discovered Halley's comet, and Sir William Herschel discovered the planet Uranus.

Many Scorpios direct the power of their emotions into artistic and creative fields, as did artists Pablo Picasso, Auguste Rodin, and Claude Monet; poets John Keats and Dylan Thomas and novelists Fyodor Dostoyevsky, Kurt Vonnegut Jr., Robert Louis Stevenson, and Nadine Gordimer; and actors Kevin Kline, F. Murray Abraham, Richard Dreyfuss, Sally Field, and Jamie Lee Curtis.

RELATIONSHIPS

The Power of Love

There is little that is halfway with you, so when you love someone, your love is total. You are loyal, and there is little you would not do for the person you care for. You are passionate in matters of love and are seeking to connect at a soul level. The bonds of love are sacred to you.

You like and respect strong people. Although you love to get your own way, you admire people who will stand up to you and demand that you give them the lead. The fact is, you understand that relationships are not always just about flowers and romance and kisses. You love the intensity, the passion, and even some of the arguments. What you do not want is a superficial relationship. You want the whole package, and you are willing to deal with everything that is involved in a deep, committed relationship.

You give your mind, heart, and soul to a relationship, and you want the person you adore to feel the same way. Lukewarm will not do, and a lack of full commitment from the other person is totally unnerving to you. But, as Scorpio Bonnie Raitt sings, "I can't make you love me if you don't/You can't make your heart feel something it won't." Learning to let go of those who do not commit as fully as you do is an act of self-empowerment. Scorpios find the right relationship when they are willing to let go of people who do not support them.

You are charismatic and alluring when you are confident. There is an aura of mystery about you that others find intriguing. People are drawn to you like a magnet. But, when you do not feel confident, you may feel jealous of any attention your loved one pays to others. These feelings relate to your trust issues. Make sure you make the distinction about who is trustworthy and who is not. Trust your instincts. Feel secure in your own lovability. Usually when you let go of trying to control your loved one, he or she comes back to you with twice the rewards.

Sign Compatibility

There are some basic concepts to keep in mind when you are thinking about compatibility. You want to remember that although Sun sign characteristics describe central and important themes in life, the Sun does not represent the *whole* person. Planets, particularly Venus, are also important to consider when determining compatibility between people. Venus is the planet that symbolizes your concept of an ideal relationship. It describes how you like to give and receive affection. The sign that Venus occupied at the time of your birth explains what is most important to you when you are in love. Other planets are equally important when it comes to relationships: Mercury is the planet that reveals your communication style; Mars is the planet of action and desire. The Moon shows your emotional temperament and security concerns.

Sun signs that are opposite each other in the zodiac are often compatible, although their personality characteristics are very different. Taurus is Scorpio's opposite sign.

Now, with these considerations in place, we can proceed!

COMPATIBILITY GUIDE

Scorpio and Aries

Life is never boring with this match! You both have energy to spare; you are both intense and passionate. You admire your Aries' strength and would go to the ends of the earth and back for her or him. You like the way Aries keeps you on your toes, and your Aries loves your intensity.

The challenge: You are both strong-willed, which can lead to plenty of arguments. Both of you will have to let the other lead sometimes to keep peace in this relationship.

Scorpio and Taurus

Taurus is your opposite sign, which brings a natural compatibility to this relationship. You love the earthy, stable vibe of a Taurus, while your Taurus finds your powerful, magnetic personality very appealing. You share the qualities of strength, loyalty, and determination, and together there is little you cannot accomplish.

The challenge: Because you are both so strong, with a tendency to be stubborn, you will have to make a point of cultivating flexibility for both of you to feel content in this relationship.

Scorpio and Gemini

You are sensitive and respond to the world through deep emotions, while a Gemini is light, airy, and lives in the world of the mind. These qualities, although very different from yours, are likely to fascinate you. Your Gemini is attracted to your intensity, while you love your Gemini's inventive mind.

The challenge: Geminis love to discuss, analyze, and chat about the things that interest them. You are less likely to want to talk about everything. You will have to sharpen your communication skills for this relationship to thrive.

Scorpio and Cancer

You are both oriented in the world of emotions and understand and respect each other's tender heart. Passion runs high in this relationship, and the intensity of your feelings for each other is strong. You both have staying power and are looking to make a deep, lasting connection.

The challenge: Your Cancer loves to take care of you, protect you, and be near you, while you prefer a little more alone time. You will both need to voice your needs to keep this relationship on track.

Scorpio and Leo

You are both strong people, which creates both attraction and fireworks. There is nothing lukewarm about this relationship! You love your Leo's loyal and fiery nature. Your Leo is drawn to your intensity and charisma. This relationship is full of passion.

The challenge: You both have a tendency to dig in your heels, refusing to budge when you think you are right. You both will have to learn how to compromise to make this relationship work.

Scorpio and Virgo

There is nothing lazy in either one of you. You respect each other's drive and intensity and enjoy the same kinds of activities. It is easy for you to fall in love with your Virgo's serious, earthy nature, while your Virgo is attracted to your strength, charisma, and charm.

The challenge: Because you both tend to be serious, it will be important to make time for fun to keep this relationship balanced.

Scorpio and Libra

You are both relationship-oriented and are looking to make a deep, soul connection with each other. You find the grace and charm of a Libra soothing, while a Libra finds your magnetic personality intriguing and appealing. You easily share your thoughts and dreams with each other.

The challenge: A Libra is quite social, whereas you like a fair amount of alone time. Strengthen your communication skills, and become more social to strengthen this relationship.

Scorpio and Scorpio

You two instinctively understand each other, have no trouble honoring the other's feelings, and know when to back off and give your loved one some space. Words do not need to tell you how tender the other's heart is. You know how to support each other's dreams.

The challenge: You both feel everything so intensely that you will want to clear up any problems that arise right away. Keeping things inside instead of talking about them can destroy what is great about this relationship.

Scorpio and Sagittarius

You are attracted to the outgoing and optimistic nature of Sagittarians. You love their philosophical take on life that helps you to cultivate faith in your own power. Sagittarians love your strength and the determination that can move mountains.

The challenge: Sagittarians are the most freedom-loving sign of the zodiac. Respect your Sagittarian's independence to help this relationship thrive.

Scorpio and Capricorn

You both are strong, serious, driven, and intense, making it easy to relate to each other. You see a kindred spirit in the other, neither of you taking life or your relationship lightly. You love your Capricorn's ambition, while your Capricorn loves your strength and loyalty.

The challenge: Although you have a lot of natural compatibility, you are both strong and like to be in charge. You will both need to allow plenty of breathing room for this relationship to flourish.

Scorpio and Aquarius

Your intense emotional nature and an Aquarian's cool detached mind make this relationship fascinating because you are so different from each other. What you share is a strong will and the courage to pave your own paths in life. One thing is for sure: neither of you will ever be bored!

The challenge: Differences can be attractive but also difficult. An Aquarian's independence is legendary, so you will need to give your Aquarius plenty of space for this relationship to take off.

Scorpio and Pisces

The two of you are psychically tuned into each other. Both from the water element, you are sensitive and have a deep instinctive understanding between you. You teach your

Pisces how to navigate the currents in life, while your Pisces teaches you all about having faith.

The challenge: You can become so focused on each other that you forget about everything else! Pay attention to the rest of your life also to make this relationship strong.

SPECIAL TIPS FOR SCORPIOS

Below are reminders and special tips that will help any Scorpio lead a successful and fulfilling life. Maximize your positive traits, and be aware of those traits that can hold you back. Make the effort to learn from your mistakes, and keep your eyes on the stars!

1. Center in your power.
2. Be a phoenix.
3. Create options; perceive choices.
4. Always have someone in your life whom you trust.
5. Be a good influence on others and associate with people who are a positive influence on you.
6. With any dilemma or situation in which you feel trapped, list five possible solutions.
7. Let go.
8. Set goals.
9. Honor your privacy.
10. Seek out activities where you can be in charge.

You, dear Scorpio, are an influencer. Choose wisely what kind of influence you want to have on others and in the world. Your determination will help you to succeed in whatever direction you want your life to take you. Your gift is power. If you own it and use it wisely, you will always have an interesting and extraordinary life.

*

Sagittarius

The Explorer
November 22 to December 21

Symbol: The Archer
Ruling planet: Jupiter
Element: Fire—*outgoing, enthusiastic, strong*
Mode: Mutable—*adaptable, changeable, restless*
Birthstone: Turquoise
Colors: Purple and dark blue

FAMOUS SAGITTARIANS:

November 22	Jesse Colin Young	November 29	Louisa May Alcott
November 23	Charles Berlitz	November 30	Shirley Chisolm
November 24	Katherine Heigl	December 1	Richard Pryor
November 25	Tina Turner	December 2	Britney Spears
November 26	Charles Schultz	December 3	Katarina Witt
November 27	Bruce Lee	December 4	Tyra Banks
November 28	William Blake	December 5	Walt Disney

December 6	Ira Gershwin	December 14	Nostradamus
December 7	Willa Cather	December 15	Don Johnson
December 8	Teri Hatcher	December 16	Jane Austen
December 9	John Malkovich	December 17	Paracelsus
December 10	Emily Dickinson	December 18	Christina Aguilera
December 11	Aleksandr Solzhenitsyn	December 19	Cicely Tyson
		December 20	Kiefer Sutherland
December 12	Tracey Austin	December 21	Jane Fonda
December 13	Dick Van Dyke		

THESE BEHAVIORS AND ATTITUDES
INCREASE CONFIDENCE

Honesty
Optimism
Enthusiasm
Intuition
Humor
Philosophical nature
Freedom-loving aspect

THESE BEHAVIORS AND ATTITUDES
DECREASE CONFIDENCE

Irresponsibility
Carelessness
Tactlessness
Preachiness
Overcommitment
Childishness
Impracticality

THE EXPLORER

You, dear Sagittarius, are the explorer of the zodiac. Your symbol, the archer, depicts a centaur, a mythical being who is half horse and half human and shoots an arrow toward the stars. A seeker, you, too, are aiming for the stars. Sagittarians travel out into the world, searching for truth and for understanding. You are a visionary on a quest. You wonder, "What am I doing here? Is there a purpose for me, a dream to follow?"

Many Sagittarians are famous for their explorations. Anthropologist Margaret Mead researched the cultures of the South Pacific and is recognized as one of the foremost anthropologists of the twentieth century. Science-fiction writer Arthur C. Clarke wrote about the frontiers of space. The movie *2001: A Space Odyssey,* based on his book of the same title, earned him worldwide recognition. Walt Disney delved into the world of animation, creating countless cartoon figures, including Mickey Mouse and Donald Duck. Scott Joplin, Grover Washington Jr., and Jimi Hendrix explored the language of music. As you can see, exploration into new or uncharted territory can be in any area. Your thirst for knowledge and experience will take you on many amazing journeys throughout your life.

Not much of a homebody, you are interested in seeing the world outside of your neighborhood. You are amazingly open to new experiences and are not afraid of differences in people. In fact, you embrace those differences. As far as you are concerned, diversity is what makes people and life exciting. You are drawn to people of different ages, races, religions, and philosophies.

You are eager to discover all there is to know about the world. Some Sagittarians are born into families who travel to different areas of the country or world, bringing them into contact with a variety of people and experiences. Some Sagittarians take advantage of foreign exchange programs in order to travel. Some participate in school trips. Some visit relatives who live far away. For most Sagittarians the excitement and love of travel begins early in life.

Some Sagittarians travel with their mind. You love to read; you tune into television travel channels to learn about people from different countries. You read *National Geographic* or books on topics about different areas the world. Many writers are Sagittarians who explore the world through literature. Jane Austen began writing plays when she was fifteen years old, and by twenty-one, she had begun to write novels. Willa Cather won acclaim for her stories about the pioneering spirit of the people of the American frontier. Aleksandr Solzhenitsyn became famous for writing about life inside the Soviet prison system. These authors introduced their readers to new worlds.

Most Sagittarians like to be on the move, whether it's by bicycle, skateboard, or Rollerblades. You are restless when you are not in motion. Because of this, many Sagittarians are drawn to sports. Some of the best-known sports figures are Sagittarians, including baseball player Joe DiMaggio, gymnast Cathy Rigby, figure skater Katarina Witt, basketball player Larry Bird, and tennis players Monica Seles and Tracey Austin.

Freedom: The Sky's the Limit!

Just as the horse (or centaur) requires wide open space to roam, you also need plenty of room to breathe and move. It is hard for you to have fences, rules, or restrictions placed on you. You are happiest when you can let your body, mind, and spirit travel anywhere they want to go. This is particularly challenging when you are young and need to follow the rules of your parents and teachers. It is important for you to find ways to fulfill your strong need for freedom within the current structure of your life.

Some Sagittarians satisfy their desire for freedom through foreign-exchange programs, giving them the opportunity to broaden their horizons and investigate other cultures. Some get involved in extracurricular activities or sports programs at their schools. For others, community programs provide an outlet. Many churches sponsor programs that give people the opportunity to engage in a variety of activities and travels. Make it a priority to fulfill your need to explore, search, ramble, and roam. Make use of the opportunities around you.

The Optimism of a Visionary

You are naturally philosophical about life. Something inside of you knows that everything will turn out for the best—or at least the way it is meant to. You are always gazing at the next horizon, the next adventure. Your innate optimism helps you through difficult passages in life. The uncanny ability to dust yourself off and start over again leads you into many areas other people wouldn't even consider. Because of your enthusiasm and ability to land on your feet, you tend to create life circumstances where people magically appear from the wings, waiting to help you out just when you need it the most.

Your optimism also gives you a great sense of humor. You have the ability to laugh at life and at yourself just when you need it the most. Many comedians are Sagittarians, including three who share the same birthday, December 1: Bette Midler, Richard Pryor, and Woody Allen.

You have a natural tendency to think BIG. Sagittarius is a sign that is forward-looking, visionary, and future-oriented. Sagittarius Branch Rickey devised the farm-team system of training baseball players and hired the first African-American players, including Jackie Robinson, in major-league baseball. Steven Spielberg is one of the most visionary filmmakers of our time. The force and power of his imagination prompt him to make films that are exciting and unique. Michel de Nostradamus's prophecies, written in the sixteenth century, are still talked about today. You, too, are a visionary. Stay true to your vision of where you want to go, what you want to seek, and what you want to accomplish. Like the centaur, aim for the stars.

From the Stars to the Earth: Taking Care of the Details of Earthly Living

Gazing at the stars, Sagittarians sometimes forget to take care of all of those little earthly details. Your ability to see the big picture (the forest rather than the trees) is one of your gifts. But, to bring balance into your life, you need to pay attention to the steps that will help you on your travels. Although the human half of the centaur is looking toward the future, to the road ahead, the centaur's body is a horse with hooves that are firmly on the ground. The combination of human and horse is what makes the centaur an image of wholeness. And for you, too, balance and wholeness requires paying just as much attention to the details of earthly living and being practical as to your adventurous quests. With only half of your centaur nature, you have a hard time providing the foundation necessary to accomplish your dreams. With the two halves together, there is little that you cannot accomplish.

A lack of attention to the particulars or details can also cause you to overcommit or to make a promise that is hard to keep. Although you really do mean it at the time when you tell somebody you will do something, once you are off to your next adventure, your promises may soon be forgotten. Think carefully before you make a commitment, or make fewer commitments. One of your challenges is to make sure that you fulfill your promises.

Honesty: The Truth, the Whole Truth, and Nothing but the Truth

You cannot figure out why people don't just tell the truth. It seems so simple to you. You are the most comfortable when all of the cards are on the table. You would rather hear something bad than nothing at all or a lie designed to make you comfortable.

You are basically an honest person and have no trouble telling people the truth. However, sometimes people have a hard time hearing what you have to tell them because you can be so blunt that you can hurt their feelings. Sagittarians need to learn that while honesty is a priority, so are people's feelings. Remember to temper your truthfulness with sensitivity. Compassion is the perfect complement to honesty.

Your Soul Mission: Examining Your Beliefs

Sagittarius, one of your best traits is your ability to inspire people. You help people to believe in themselves; you encourage them to reach for the stars. Your optimism about your own life helps people be optimistic about themselves and their lives, too. Keep in mind, as you are encouraging people, that there is a difference between being on a soapbox and just plain inspiring folks to do better. Thinking that you know what is best for others can cause you problems.

You have strong beliefs about right and wrong, which help you establish the moral code by which you live. And, even though you are often wise, you are not always right—even when you think you are! Being overly attached to your beliefs and thinking that your opinions are always the right ones are issues with which most Sagittarians have to grapple.

As a seeker, you are interested in knowing the truth—about yourself, others, and existence itself. And, once you have discovered something that seems true, you are eager to share it. Sharing your knowledge is important. It is also important to respect the beliefs and views of others. Make sure you do not try to convince people of the "rightness" of your opinions. Instead, focus on your appreciation of the diversity of human experience.

Your beliefs about yourself, others, and the world form the foundation of your life. Analyze the effect of your beliefs. If they make you feel confident, you are building a strong foundation from which much success will result. If your beliefs undermine or weaken you or others, they need to be reexamined. Believe in your own and others' greatness. That belief will lead you to success.

FRIENDSHIP

Your friends are likely to be an interesting assortment of people. Many of these folks, if they were ever to meet, may not even like one another or have much to talk about. You are the common denominator. Your attraction to diversity shows up in your choice of friends. They may resemble a mini–United Nations! Your friends are a wonderful source for learning about the world. And, because of your open and friendly nature, people are naturally drawn to you.

You love to go exploring, so activities with friends where you are out doing things are the most fun—such as going to the movies or a concert, hanging out in the park, skateboard-ing, or going for a bike ride. Sitting around the house is not your favorite thing to do.

Honesty between you and your friends is a requirement. It bothers you if people are not truthful or keep a lot hidden. Intrigue and secrecy does not attract you. Instead, the bonds of friendship are strengthened by direct, straightforward communication.

Check out the compatibility guide later in this chapter to see how your friends' Sun signs match up with yours.

HOME LIFE

You are the roving ambassador of your family. You are the person who will travel out into the world and bring the out-side world back to their doorstep. Don't be concerned if your family doesn't understand this need to explore. It is your job as a good Sagittarius to be a seeker—not theirs. Many Sagit-tarians live in areas, states, or countries other than where they were born. American-born Tina Turner chose to settle down in France. Bruce Lee, another famous Sagittarius, was born in the United States but raised in Hong Kong. He later moved back to the land of his birth, bringing his Asian cul-ture with him as he instructed people in martial arts.

Your room should have posters of different countries or photo albums with pictures from your travels. A box for all of your projects (the half-finished ones) will keep them together for when you are ready to work on them again. Your sleeping bag and backpack should be where you can grab them at a moment's notice. Since you love a feeling of space, a big room or windows that allow plenty of light feels the best.

CAREER

A job that offers you room to move and plenty of freedom would be the most suitable. Or, you may want to work in a profession where you can make your own hours. A nine-to-five job sitting at the same desk for eight hours a day, forty hours a week, is not for you!

You may enjoy a job that promotes travel, such as working for a travel or tour company. Or, you may be interested in becoming an airline pilot or train engineer. Interest in other countries and languages may lead you to become a translator. Sagittarius Charles Berlitz started his own language schools, making the world's languages accessible to the ordinary citizen.

Your love of knowledge and learning may take you into literary circles. Plenty of writers populate your sign, including Louisa May Alcott, C. S. Lewis, Rainer Maria Rilke, and Emily Dickinson.

As you are a visionary, exploring new frontiers comes naturally to you. Sagittarius actor, director, and producer Kenneth Branagh's vision led him to introduce Shakespeare's plays to new audiences.

Comedian Richard Pryor took the Sagittarius habit of telling the truth and revolutionized comedy with his funny and poignant stories. Shirley Chisolm's campaign slogan "Unbought and Unbossed" helped her to become the first black woman ever elected to the United States Congress. Just like values of the above Sagittarians, your ethics are a guiding force in your life. Your desire to tell your truth can guide you to any profession that sparks your passion.

RELATIONSHIPS

Love Inspires

Above all, when you are in love, you give your whole heart. You love enthusiastically. You make grand declarations of your affection. You are fun to be with, you make people laugh, and you inspire them. You are memorable to everyone you meet.

You enjoy philosophical discussions and sharing your dreams for the future with your loved one. You have a great time with open-minded people who are as fearless as you are—people who are fun and can be adventure pals who travel to parts unknown. You love to laugh, so someone who has a great sense of humor is very attractive to you.

You value your freedom so highly, you would think that you would be attracted to someone who has those needs at the top of their list, too. Although some Sagittarians are drawn to people who are similar to them, many are attracted to those who are much more practical than they are. If you were with someone who liked to explore and wander as much as you do, you two may never find each other again after your first date! Yes, you like someone who is okay with *your* need to travel and roam, but you love people who have their feet on the ground. This doesn't mean you want someone who is afraid to walk out of the front door, but it is comforting for you to know that you are with someone who has a feel for the nuts and bolts of practical living.

Sagittarians who balance their need for freedom with forming close, meaningful relationships find that love provides an unshakable foundation. To help you maintain this balance, make sure that you are not leaving all of the material, practical things in life for your loved one to manage. Keep track of your stuff, and follow through with your promises to establish a loving, enduring relationship.

Sign Compatibility

There are some basic concepts to keep in mind when you are thinking about compatibility. You want to remember that although Sun sign characteristics describe central and important themes in life, the Sun does not represent the *whole* person. Planets, particularly Venus, are also important to consider when determining compatibility between people Venus is the planet that symbolizes your concept of an ideal relationship. It describes how you like to give and receive affection. The sign that Venus occupied at the time of your birth explains what is most important to you when you are in love. Other planets are equally important when it comes to relationships: Mercury is the planet that reveals your communication style; Mars is the planet of action and desire. The Moon shows your emotional temperament and security concerns.

Sun signs that are opposite each other in the zodiac are often compatible, although their personality characteristics are very different. Gemini is Sagittarius's opposite sign.

Now, with these considerations in place, we can proceed!

COMPATIBILITY GUIDE

Sagittarius and Aries

Independence and freedom are important to you both. This deep understanding and respect for the independence of the other is what makes this relationship magical. You are both courageous and idealistic, and there is little you cannot or will not do when you are with each other.

The challenge: Because you are both freedom-loving people, make a point to travel together to keep this relationship strong.

Sagittarius and Taurus

There are many Sagittarius/Taurus couples. You love the loyalty, dependability, and earthiness of a Taurus. A Taurus loves your outgoing nature and the excitement you bring to the relationship. This is an example where your different personalities can add to the fullness and richness of life.

The challenge: You like the excitement of a new adventure, whereas a Taurus is more comfortable with predictability. Adapt to each other's style to help this relationship succeed.

Sagittarius and Gemini

Gemini is your opposite sign, which creates natural compatibility. You love the clever, witty mind and playful personality of your Gemini. Gemini loves your sense of humor and optimism. Your connection is effortless, making it easy to support and understand each other.

The challenge: Although both of you need plenty of room to breathe, make sure your independent natures do not take you in opposite directions.

Sagittarius and Cancer

You each respond to life differently, which is what holds the attraction between you. You respect the instincts and feelings of a Cancer as much as he or she loves your intuitive nature. A Cancer is protective of you and provides a safe haven to come back to after your adventures.

The challenge: Whereas you love to be on the go, a Cancer is a homebody, loving the comfort and security of the familiar. Accommodate each other to keep this relationship on track.

Sagittarius and Leo

Life is fun and dramatic when you are with a Leo. Both fire signs, you are passionate people and have big ideas about where you are going and what you want to do. Because you are generous, loving, and supportive of each other, it is easy to keep the magic going in this relationship.

The challenge: Although the two of you know how to have fun together, you are the more adventurous one. Make sure your travels don't take you so far that you lose your connection with your Leo.

Sagittarius and Virgo
With your big dreams and Virgo's high standards and expectations in life, there is nothing the two of you can't do! You share an idealistic nature and are ready to make your mark on the world. A Virgo has the practical common sense that helps make your dreams come true.

The challenge: A Virgo's practicality can either ground you or irritate you. Be tolerant of and appreciate the differences in your personalities to make this relationship work.

Sagittarius and Libra
A Libra's diplomatic nature and love of fairness and justice really appeals to you. Your Libra appreciates your sense of humor, your philosophical mind, and your honesty. Comfortable together, you find it easy to support each other and to help each other fulfill your dreams.

The challenge: You are independent and need plenty of freedom, while a Libra enjoys spending more time together. Include your Libra in your travels to keep your connection strong.

Sagittarius and Scorpio
A Scorpio brings emotional depth and intensity to a relationship, which you find intriguing. Your Scorpio is drawn to your outgoing and optimistic nature. Here, different styles complement each other, providing different ways of experiencing the world.

The challenge: You like to meet new people and seek novel experiences. Your Scorpio doesn't crave the adventure that you do; he or she has a reserved nature and likes to be more private. Appreciating these differences will help this relationship thrive.

Sagittarius and Sagittarius

Nobody understands you better than another Sagittarius. You love to explore the world together, and you respect each other's need for freedom. Honesty is at the top of both of your lists of values, so there is nothing that you cannot share with each other.

The challenge: Make sure you travel together to keep your connection with each other close.

Sagittarius and Capricorn

You both aspire to great things, making it easy for you to support each other's ideals and dreams. A Capricorn's seriousness complements your more outgoing nature. You inspire your Capricorn, while he or she helps you keep your feet on the ground.

The challenge: You need much more freedom than a Capricorn may be comfortable with. Spend time doing things your Capricorn enjoys to keep this relationship strong.

Sagittarius and Aquarius

You both love your freedom and independence, so neither of you will try to hold the other back. Life is exciting and fun and often an adventure when you are together. You find an Aquarian's unpredictability intriguing. An Aquarius loves your optimistic approach to life.

The challenge: Because both of you are so independent, make sure you spend enough time together to help this relationship flourish.

Sagittarius and Pisces

You are both dreamers and idealists at heart, which creates a powerful connection between you. With your intuition and a

Pisces' psychic abilities, you often do not need words to express your affection for each other.

The challenge: You love to go out exploring, while your Pisces is not as adventurous as you are. Accommodate these differences to help this relationship survive.

SPECIAL TIPS FOR SAGITTARIANS

Here are some reminders and special tips that will help any Sagittarius lead a successful and fulfilling life. Maximize your positive traits, and be aware of those traits that can hold you back. Make the effort to learn from your mistakes, and keep your eyes on the stars!

1. Temper honesty with compassion.
2. Honor your need for freedom.
3. Travel when you have the opportunity.
4. Take care of the practical tasks of living so that other people are not picking up after you.
5. You can get away with a lot because you are so charming, but that does not mean that you *should*.
6. Your natural optimism is one of your best qualities. Do not let other people convince you of a gloomier version of the world.
7. Respect people's right to their beliefs.
8. In your personal relationships, it is better to be kind than to be right.
9. Throw out any beliefs that are not supportive of you or of others.
10. Think twice before you commit to something. Make sure you will be able to back up your promises.

✳

You, dear Sagittarius, are an explorer. Your travels will take you on amazing adventures throughout your life. Your natural optimism and enthusiasm will help you to discover exciting new worlds, taking you as far as you want to go. Shoot for the stars, and you will always have a rich and rewarding life.

✳

Capricorn

The Achiever
December 21 to January 20

Symbol: The Mountain Goat
Ruling planet: Saturn
Element: Earth—*practical, cautious, reliable*
Mode: Cardinal—*energetic, initiating, active*
Birthstone: Garnet
Colors: Gray and brown

FAMOUS CAPRICORN PEOPLE:

December 21	Rebecca West	December 28	Denzel Washington
December 22	Ralph Fiennes		
December 23	Susan Lucci	December 29	Paula Poundstone
December 24	Ricky Martin		
December 25	Clara Barton	December 30	Tiger Woods
December 26	Jared Leto	December 31	Elizabeth Arden
December 27	Louis Pasteur	January 1	Betsy Ross

January 2	Cuba Gooding Jr.	January 12	Kirstie Alley
January 3	Mel Gibson	January 13	Horatio Alger
January 4	Michael Stipe	January 14	Albert Schweitzer
January 5	Paramahansa Yogananda	January 15	Martin Luther King, Jr.
January 6	Joan of Arc	January 16	Dian Fossey
January 7	Nicolas Cage	January 17	Jim Carrey
January 8	Stephen Hawking	January 18	A. A. Milne
January 9	Dave Matthews	January 19	Edgar Allan Poe
January 10	Shawn Colvin	January 20	Federico Fellini
January 11	Naomi Judd		

THESE BEHAVIORS AND ATTITUDES
INCREASE CONFIDENCE

Ambition
Discipline
A sense of humor
Persistence
Self-reliance
Hard work
Responsibility

THESE BEHAVIORS AND ATTITUDES
DECREASE CONFIDENCE

Pessimism
Inhibition
Rigidity
Strictness
Authoritarian tendency
Emotional unavailability
Cynicism

THE ACHIEVER

Look for someone at the "top of the mountain," who is a leader and has accomplished something of significance, and you will find a Capricorn. You are a doer, a "mover and shaker." You aim for the stars, and, more often than not, you arrive at your destination. There are few signs in the zodiac that are as disciplined and hardworking as you are. You are willing to do what so many people are unwilling to do—to put in the effort and do what is necessary to achieve your goals. This ability will take you very far in life. Aim high and have confidence in your dreams because you have what it takes to fulfill them—you have "the right stuff."

Just like your symbol, the mountain goat, you climb up the mountain one careful step at a time. Capricorns are often those who arrive at the top of their profession and are known around the world for extraordinary achievements. Tiger Woods is one of the best golfers in the history of the sport; boxers George Foreman, Joe Frazier, and Muhammad Ali (the latter two even share the same birthday) are among the best boxers in the world. Robert Joffrey and Alvin Ailey started their own dance companies that became famous worldwide; Clara Barton founded the American Red Cross, and Elizabeth Arden built a cosmetics empire in the early twentieth century. Many of the world's most famous, talented, and respected entertainers are Capricorns, such as Elvis Presley, Janis Joplin, James Earl Jones, Mel Gibson, Sissy Spacek, Dolly Parton, and Denzel Washington. All of these Capricorns are achievers who took their dreams and went all the way with them.

Capricorns are the architects of the world. An architect is someone who designs, plans, and creates. For a Capricorn, ideas do not just stay at the thought stage. They are actually drawn up and implemented. In this regard, Capricorns tend to be excellent organizers, planners, and strategists.

As practical as Capricorns are, they are also idealistic. This is a great combination because it creates the ability to manifest a dream. Many people have a vision of what they would like to accomplish, but Capricorns are likely to achieve their vision because of their practical approach. Capricorns Alexander Hamilton and Benjamin Franklin were two of the architects of the American Constitution. Louis Braille, blinded at the age of three, devised the Braille system at age fifteen. This is the universally used system of writing for the blind. Three of the world's most brilliant scientists—physicist and mathematician Sir Isaac Newton, astronomer and astrologer Johannes Kepler, and physicist Stephen Hawking developed new theories of understanding the world and the universe. Lucretia Mott's ideas prompted her to help found the American Anti-Slavery Society in 1833 and to organize with Elizabeth Cady Stanton a women's rights convention in 1848. Martin Luther King, Jr.'s, dream gave the United States a leader of the Civil Rights Movement. Joan of Arc's visions inspired entire armies to go into battle to free France from English domination, with seventeen-year-old Joan leading the way. What is your vision? Have confidence in your incredible ability to make your dreams come true.

Responsibilities

There is an old saying "Capricorns get younger as they grow older." The basis for this is that many Capricorns learn about the importance of responsibilities earlier in life than most other signs, although the reasons for this are varied. Some of you may be the oldest child in the family and share in the care of younger siblings. Others may not have any siblings and spend more time in the company of adults than with other kids. For still others, there are conditions in the home that require more of you, such as having an ill family member. Or, maybe your mother is a single mom and needs you to chip in and help with household chores. Some Capricorns simply feel more comfortable in the adult world. Whatever the causes,

Capricorns seem to feel their responsibilities keenly and worry about everything being taken care of and managed.

No matter what conditions bring responsibilities into your life, one thing is clear: you have maturity beyond your years and can handle a lot of things earlier in life than can many other people. You are learning skills now that will contribute to your success later. Actor and comedian Jim Carrey is at the top of his profession now, but his youth was marked by poverty and hardship. He learned early in life about living within limitations and about the value of hard work. Capricorn Horatio Alger wrote a number of books about people overcoming great obstacles to become successful. Alger's name is associated with the theme of "rags to riches" success.

Because you are competent and excel at accomplishing tasks, you may have a tendency to take on others' responsibilities or do their work for them. Just because you are able to do something doesn't mean that you should. If you take on others' burdens, they will eventually weigh you down. You are an excellent role model for others. People learn from you. You inspire others to do better and to reach higher. If you do for them what they should do for themselves, you will not help them. You will hold them back. One of a Capricorn's chief lessons is to learn to delegate—to let others share the work and the responsibility.

Although one of your wonderful traits is this keen sense of duty, obligation, and responsibility toward others, one of your life tasks is to make sure that you are being responsible to yourself. Others may want something for you that you do not want for yourself. Make sure you choose a path that you want to walk.

Enjoy the Climb

It can be difficult to remain enthusiastic when working toward a long-term goal unless you think in terms of smaller steps. Ask yourself if the hard work you are putting in right now has a purpose. For example, will studying hard for a test on a subject you don't care about contribute to reaching your goal of getting into the college of your choice? Most people who have fulfilled their dreams worked hard to get there. The fact is, most Capricorns do not mind the hard work it takes to reach their goals. It is more likely that you will enjoy the process. Few things are as satisfying as the sweet pleasure of achieving something that has been hard won.

Authority: Being in Charge

You are learning how to be in charge and are likely to end up in leadership positions throughout your life. What makes someone a good authority figure? You are learning this as you observe your teachers, your parents, your clergy, your coach, or your boss. What would you do the same or differently? How do people act when they feel secure in their authority? How about the ones who don't feel so confident? Since you are likely to end up in a position of authority, try to observe without becoming judgmental. Being in charge is not an easy position to be in because it is so visible! Everyone sees all of your mistakes as well as those things that you do well. Someday when you are the authority figure, you will feel grateful when people understand that you are doing your best.

Is the Glass Half Empty or Half Full?

All Capricorns need to pay attention to the difference between being pessimistic and being realistic. Since Capricorns notice the things in the world that are not working well along with those things that are, there are times when they may feel discouraged. Make sure you don't develop a cynical attitude toward life and people—thinking about and seeing the worst qualities in people instead of the best. Or thinking about the hardest aspects of living, instead of the most rewarding. If you feel this way, take the steps to bring more fulfilling experiences into your life to help you cultivate a more optimistic outlook. Martin Luther King, Jr., could not have led the Civil Rights Movement if he had been cynical about human nature. Since you are an earth sign, do something concrete and tangible to restore your faith in people and the world. Roll up your sleeves, cultivate that can-do attitude, and allow your inspirations to guide you.

The Picture inside the Frame

Capricorns have an exceptional gift for understanding the world and are unusually attuned to the social hierarchy (who is on top and who isn't). You notice how people dress and behave, who is successful, who is popular, and whether people have a good or bad reputation. This attunement may, at times, keep you so focused on appearances that you forget about the inner reality of a situation. It's like noticing the beautiful frame around a painting and forgetting to look at the painting itself. Obviously no matter how good something or someone looks on the outside, that does not tell you what is going on inside. Perhaps you've heard the saying "Don't judge a book by its cover."

For example, just because someone is an honor student doesn't mean that he or she has it all together and has no worries. The most popular boy in school is not necessarily the happiest. If your friend lives in a beautiful house with both parents and a new car, it doesn't mean that the family is trouble-free.

The same holds true for you. You may be so focused on outer achievements that you forget to pay attention to how you *feel* about what you are doing. Success and happiness go together only when you make a point of being true to your feelings and doing what is right for you. That way, both the frame and the picture are beautiful. They are a perfect fit.

Your Soul Mission: Uniting the Material and Spiritual Worlds

As with any earth-sign person who is acclimated to the material world, it is not this world that is a mystery to you but the world of the unseen. Does something exist if I can't taste, touch, smell, hear, or see it? Your symbol, the goat, is sometimes depicted as the goat/fish. This symbol for Capricorn combines the earth plane with the unseen, or spiritual, world. It is the combination that cultivates the deep wisdom that is your birthright. But, it is up to every Capricorn to decide whether or not to explore beyond the physical world.

Many spiritual leaders and philosophers are Capricorns. Paramahansa Yogananda traveled from India to America in 1920 to teach Americans meditation, yoga, and how to live a more spiritual life. His book *Autobiography of a Yogi* is one of the classics of spiritual literature. Evangeline Booth, daughter of William Booth, who founded the Salvation Army, carried on her father's vision and became one of the Salvation Army's most effective leaders. Kahlil Gibran, a mystic poet and author of *The Prophet,* is still inspiring people today. Albert Schweitzer, a minister, a musician, a doctor, and a philosopher, was not only immensely practical, but was a deeply spiritual man who believed that reverence for all life was the key to understanding the human mind and spirit.

It is from the top of the mountain that the landscape is most clearly seen. When we are in the valleys and cannot see beyond the mountains, we may think that nothing is worth the climb. Although Capricorns have the gift of knowing how to travel though the valleys and mountains of life, the view from the top offers a larger picture. That view has served as an inspiration for many Capricorns.

So, make sure you do not get stuck in the foothills where it is easy to get depressed or to feel hopeless. If you become cynical and judgmental about your possibilities in life and the road in front of you looks dreary, put on your hiking boots and climb to the top of the mountain where you can see everything clearly.

FRIENDSHIP

Capricorns take friendship seriously. You do not seek superficial relationships but instead are interested in forming strong, lasting bonds that deepen and strengthen over time. Your friends may seek you out for advice. You often help them achieve their goals because of your practical know-how and wisdom about the world.

For you, age is not a barrier to making friends. In fact, you are likely to have friends of all ages, and, because of your maturity, may be particularly drawn to those who are older than you.

Cautious and sometimes shy, you tend to choose your friends carefully and prefer to let a friendship develop over time. Some people may mistake your reserved manner for a lack of interest in others, although nothing could be further from the truth. Make sure you reach out in a friendly way so that people are aware that you would like to get to know them.

You do well in positions of authority, so school clubs or activities where you can be in a leadership role provides a great environment for you to build your confidence and meet new people.

Being tuned into the social hierarchy, you can be very status conscious. To create a full and rewarding social life, explore friendship possibilities from a variety of groups.

Check out the compatibility guide later in this chapter to see how your friends' Sun signs match up with yours.

HOME LIFE

How you think about and approach your family and home life is crucial. You are being groomed for success by learning now what many people never learn or find out about much later in life—how to treat life seriously and take care of your responsibilities. Your feelings and attitudes toward your family help define how you approach your future. Expecting the best of yourself builds immeasurable confidence and paves the way to your success in life.

You are probably private when it comes to discussing your thoughts and feelings with your parents or guardians.

Sometimes, you simply don't want to reveal your feelings. But other times, you may not know what you are feeling. Get to know yourself! Writing in a journal is a good way to keep in touch with what is going on inside of you.

Many Capricorns have jobs when they are young. You love to be self-sufficient and want to grow up fast. Having an after-school or weekend job gives you confidence in your abilities while earning the respect of family members.

You are most likely to be comfortable in a bedroom that is more simply furnished, with your belongings organized so that you know where you can find them. Keep a journal in your room to list your goals and record your thoughts and dreams. Keep track of both your outer achievements and your inner life. Posters or photographs of people you admire—or even of a mountain—are perfect images for you to see every day.

CAREER

You are a realist when it comes to your working life. You instinctively understand that hard work, discipline, and persistence pay off. You are prepared to enter the job market and work your way up. You are not looking for a free ride, so you do not sit around idly and daydream about where you want to go in life. You do well working within organizations and enjoy the structure that they provide as long as there is an upward path. Many Capricorns choose self-employment in order to maintain control over their working life.

Although Capricorns choose many different careers, what they have in common is that most want to reach the top of their profession—and often do. Many have been mentioned earlier in this chapter. Others include Capricorns Diane Sawyer and Cokie Roberts, who are two of the best in broadcast journalism; Edgar Allan Poe and Rudyard Kipling, who figure among the finest writers; and Cuba Gooding Jr. and Robert Duvall, who express themselves as talented actors. As you can see, Capricorns are in many professions. What they

share are the qualities of persistence and drive. *How* you climb
to the top is just as important as arriving. Capricorn former
president Richard Nixon learned that lesson the hard way.
Keep true to your values as you climb the ladder of success.

RELATIONSHIPS

The Beauty of Commitment

Most Capricorns do not like to jump into relationships. You
are more comfortable taking your time getting to know
someone. You may even be a little shy and reserved. You
don't treat love frivolously and are not interested in superficial relationships. When you give your heart to someone, it is
a sacred act. You are looking to see what you and the person
you care for can build together.

You prefer knowing people's intentions before you let
them know how you feel. Are they just looking to play
around, or are they serious about you? It may be unnerving
for you to go through the process of getting to know someone
without being sure how it will all turn out.

Keep tuned into your feelings about your relationship.
The outer picture may look so good, with friends and family
just loving your sweetheart, that you forget to pay enough
attention to whether or not *you* like that person. He or she
may act great in public and be totally different when you are
alone together. To create a fulfilling relationship, stay in
touch with your emotions. They will guide you in making
the choices that are right for you.

You are so together and have so much of life handled that
you may be attracted to someone who is extrasensitive or
emotional. You love someone whom you can protect and do
things for. But, make sure you don't try to be in control or in
charge of the relationship, or you will end up doing all of the
work for both of you.

You may be attracted to those wild types and then want to
tame them (a losing battle!). Instead, allow them to bring out the

playful side in you. Mel Gibson is a great example of a Capricorn who keeps work and play in balance. He is known as a "big kid" who delights in playing practical jokes on his friends. But, he is also a family man with fairly traditional values.

Because Capricorns are often more mature than their chronological age, you may find yourself attracted to someone who is a little older than you. You are looking for a partner who is grown up enough to relate in a mature manner and who is interested in building a lasting relationship.

Sign Compatibility

There are some basic concepts to keep in mind when you are thinking about compatibility. You want to remember that although Sun sign characteristics describe central and important themes in life, the Sun does not represent the *whole* person. Planets, particularly Venus, are also important to consider when determining compatibility between people. Venus is the planet that symbolizes your concept of an ideal relationship. It describes how you like to give and receive affection. The sign that Venus occupied at the time of your birth explains what is most important to you when you are in love. Other planets are equally important when it comes to relationships: Mercury is the planet that reveals your communication style; Mars is the planet of action and desire. The Moon shows your emotional temperament and security concerns.

Signs that are opposite each other in the zodiac are often compatible, although their personality characteristics are very different. Cancer is Capricorn's opposite sign.

Now, with these considerations in place, we can proceed!

COMPATIBILITY GUIDE

Capricorn and Aries

Aries people are impulsive and feisty, which may be both attractive and a little unnerving to you. An Aries brings out the kid in you, is fun to be with, and definitely keeps you on your toes! In turn, your Aries loves how strong and grounded you are.

The challenge: You will have to resist the urge to control the spontaneity and sometimes-reckless behavior of your Aries for this relationship to last.

Capricorn and Taurus
Both earth signs, you are cautious and like to take your time getting to know each other. Your Taurus instinctively understands you and is as serious as you are when it comes to love and commitment. Your personalities are complementary, which makes it easy to appreciate and support each other.

The challenge: Because a Taurus moves at a slower pace than you do, don't rush your Taurus if you want this relationship to grow.

Capricorn and Gemini
The lighthearted nature of a Gemini intrigues you, and a Gemini is fascinated by your stable, serious personality. You help keep your Gemini's feet on the ground, while your Gemini helps make your life interesting. Both of you have a great sense of humor, which can help keep your relationship on track.

The challenge: Geminis need plenty of conversation to keep them interested. Make sure you take time to chat to help this relationship thrive.

Capricorn and Cancer
Cancer is your opposite sign, which sparks a natural attraction. The strong emotional life and nurturing instincts of a Cancer can be a magnet for you. You are both content to let this relationship develop over time. It is easy to feel comfortable and secure in this relationship.

The challenge: Cancers are so feelings-oriented that you will need to be sensitive to your Cancer's emotional life to keep this relationship growing.

Capricorn and Leo

Although your personalities are very different, you share an aura of authority and strength that is very appealing to both of you. You are both passionate and idealistic—although you are much more practical in your approach to life than is your Leo.

The challenge: Leos thrive on having fun, whereas you are more serious. You will need to appreciate your Leo's sense of drama and set aside plenty of recreational time to keep this relationship strong.

Capricorn and Virgo

Both earth signs, you instinctively understand each other. You share a commonsense approach to life, which makes it easy to spend time together. Your Virgo supports your goals and understands your dreams. You appreciate your Virgo's can-do attitude.

The challenge: Since both of you are doers, make sure you are working on something jointly, or you may find yourself so busy with separate activities that you can't find time to spend together.

Capricorn and Libra

You love the diplomatic, gracious personality of a Libra, while Libras love your earthy and ambitious nature. You are both dreamers and idealists at heart. Your Libra is very supportive of you and knows just how to make your life easier.

The challenge: Libras like to spend a lot of time with those they care for, while you are fine with maintaining more distance. You will need to invest time in this relationship to maintain harmony.

Capricorn and Scorpio

Both of you are serious and somewhat intense, so you easily find a friend in each other. Scorpios are determined and loyal—qualities you identify with and appreciate. Your Scorpio's privacy needs will need to be honored, while your Scorpio will have to learn to open up and trust you.

The *challenge:* Because you are both strong and like to be in charge, you will need to learn to work together to make this relationship flourish.

Capricorn and Sagittarius

You both aspire to great things, which makes it is easy for you to support each other's ideals and dreams, although you are much more practical in your approach. A Sagittarian's ability to throw caution to the wind intrigues you, while your ambitiousness is attractive to a Sagittarius.

The *challenge:* While you are a realist about the hard work required to attain your dreams, your Sagittarius relies on optimism and faith. Adjust to these differences to help this relationship stay on course.

Capricorn and Capricorn

Two serious souls heading for success creates an exceptional and enduring relationship. You are on the same wavelength and are content to allow your relationship to deepen over time. Acceptance, love, and support come easily.

The *challenge:* Because you both are ambitious and hardworking, make sure you take time to play to bring balance to this relationship.

Capricorn and Aquarius

The quirky independence of an Aquarius is intriguing to you. While you tend to be more reserved and cautious, your Aquarian's style is to be as original as possible. Aquarians are attracted to your earthy personality, while you love the way an Aquarius can loosen you up!

The *challenge:* An Aquarian's independent style may be a lot for you to handle. Be ready to be pulled out of your comfort zone for this relationship to last.

Capricorn and Pisces

A Pisces is sensitive, empathetic, giving, and knows just how to soothe your nerves. This water/earth combination brings together two kindred souls. Your Pisces loves your strength, while you find it easy to appreciate your Pisces' dreams and goals.

The challenge: A Pisces tends to be more laid-back than you are. Take time to relax and just "be" with your Pisces for contentment to reign in this relationship.

SPECIAL TIPS FOR CAPRICORNS

Below are some reminders and special tips that will help any Capricorn lead a successful and fulfilling life. Maximize your positive traits, and be aware of those traits that can hold you back. Make the effort to learn from your mistakes, and keep your eyes on the stars!

1. Don't take on other people's responsibilities.
2. Aim high, and success is yours.
3. Don't be so focused on your goals that you don't care how you reach them.
4. Take time to play.
5. Keep the material world and your spiritual life in balance.
6. Stay in touch with your feelings.
7. Don't mistake pessimism for being realistic.
8. Take in the view from the top of the mountain to keep the larger picture in mind.
9. Step into positions of authority.
10. Don't judge a book by its cover.

You, dear Capricorn, are an achiever, a builder, and an architect. Through your choices you are designing the blueprint for your life. Let nothing stop you when you want to achieve something. At their highest and fullest expression, your Capricorn traits can help you climb any mountain you desire.

✳

Aquarius

The Free Spirit
January 20 to February 19

Symbol: The Water Bearer
Ruling planet: Uranus
Element: Air—*social, communicative, detached*
Mode: Fixed—*determined, loyal, stubborn*
Birthstone: Amethyst
Color: Turquoise

FAMOUS AQUARIUS PEOPLE:

January 20	Bill Mahr	January 26	Ellen DeGeneres
January 21	Geena Davis	January 27	Wolfgang Amadeus
January 22	André-Marie		Mozart
	Ampère	January 28	Sarah McLachlan
January 23	Tiffani-Amber	January 29	Oprah Winfrey
	Thiessen	January 30	Phil Collins
January 24	Mary Lou Retton	January 31	Justin Timberlake
January 25	Etta James	February 1	Langston Hughes

February 2	James Joyce	February 11	Jennifer Aniston
February 3	James Michener	February 12	Abraham Lincoln
February 4	Rosa Parks	February 13	Peter Gabriel
February 5	Jennifer Jason Leigh	February 14	Frederick Douglass
February 6	Natalie Cole	February 15	Susan B. Anthony
February 7	Chris Rock	February 16	John McEnroe
February 8	Seth Green	February 17	Michael Jordon
February 9	Alice Walker	February 18	Toni Morrison
February 10	Laura Dern	February 19	Brad Steiger

THESE BEHAVIORS AND ATTITUDES INCREASE CONFIDENCE

Independence
Originality
Humanitarianism
Friendliness
Inventiveness
Progressiveness
Freedom-loving nature

THESE BEHAVIORS AND ATTITUDES DECREASE CONFIDENCE

Rebelliousness
Inflexibility
Aloofness
Insensitivity
Intolerance
Opinionatedness
Stubborness

THE FREE SPIRIT

Nobody sees the world quite the way you do. You are a free spirit with a totally original take on life. Your uniqueness is one of your outstanding features. You have a rare ability to stay tuned into your own vision even when other people do not see things the same way. This quality has given the world some of its most brilliant and innovative thinkers. You are not here to blend in and be like everyone else. Like a salmon swimming upstream, you are moving in a different direction. In this world, to manifest your own exceptional vision of life, you are progressive and future-oriented. You don't do things quite the way everybody else does, nor accept something just because others do. You march to the beat of your own drum. You are one of the leaders bringing the rest of humanity into the Aquarian Age.

Aquarius Rosa Parks sparked the Civil Rights movement when she marched to the beat of her own drum by refusing to give up her bus seat to a white man. Susan B. Anthony fought tirelessly for a woman's right to vote during a time when women had few legal rights. More than half a century later, author and activist Betty Friedan challenged the traditional roles of women and cofounded the National Organization for Women. Frederick Douglass, an escaped slave, became a leading abolitionist, inspiring many through his writing and speeches. He was also a passionate advocate for women's rights. Nicolaus Copernicus's premise that Earth revolved around the Sun countered the prevailing theory of his time. Fellow Aquarius Galileo challenged much of the scientific thought of his day and was placed under house arrest for teaching the Copernican doctrine. All of these Aquarians are some of the greatest innovators and thinkers the world has ever seen.

Many Aquarians are memorable simply because they stand out as people who are unlike anybody else. There has never been a basketball player like Aquarius Michael Jordan. His talent is that unusual. Composer Wolfgang Amadeus Mozart stunned people with his extraordinary talent. Oprah Winfrey is a phenomenon. Her success has made her one of the wealthiest women in the world. And, in true Aquarian fashion, she has introduced countless people to new ways of thinking about their lives while encouraging them to help others.

Many Aquarians fall into one of two types. The first kind is more social, people-oriented, and outgoing. Friendliness, being a member of a group, being social, and being with people is important. If you fit this type, you will make a point of meeting new people and joining school clubs and activities.

The second kind of Aquarius is more private. If you are this type, you are like the inventor or scientist who is able to work long hours alone. You are less concerned with exploring the social world or involving yourself in common causes. Instead, you enjoy expressing yourself through solitary activities such as doing research, spending time at your computer, writing, or painting. For you, socializing may feel exhausting.

A large number of Aquarians are a combination of both of these types: sometimes going to the movies with friends or to a party, and other times just wanting to be alone with their thoughts and dreams.

Question Authority

You do not like to do anything just because somebody told you to do it. Rules need to make sense to you before you will follow them. When people take the time to explain why they are asking you to do something, you are more likely to cooperate. You like to be self-reliant and to make your own decisions. Your independence and freedom are important, and you guard them fiercely. You have the strength of your convictions and act on principle.

When you are in touch with your motivations, rebelliousness can turn into something strong and purposeful. Rebelliousness can mean being stubborn or acting out just for the sake of not wanting anybody to tell you what to do. Purposefulness is having an important goal or intention that is based on principles that provide a basis for your opinions. Make sure you know what is important to you and why. Let your values and principles be your guide.

The Water Bearer

Aquarius is often mistaken for a water sign (a sign of feelings) rather than an air sign (a sign of the mind) because the Aquarius symbol is the Water Bearer. Although the Water Bearer pours water from an urn, the water is symbolic of consciousness or knowledge. This symbol, unlike most others in the zodiac, is human rather than animal and represents the mental faculties—those things that can be understood intellectually. The Water Bearer symbolizes the illumination and knowledge that come from the heavens. The story of Prometheus, who stole fire from the gods in order to bring it to humankind, has been linked with your sign, following the concept that the gifts of the gods can be brought to Earth to benefit people. This is a role that many Aquarians have undertaken both by introducing new social ideas and philosophies and through inventions.

Prometheus brought fire. Aquarius Thomas Edison brought us the electric lightbulb and the phonograph, along with more than a thousand other patented inventions. André-Marie Ampère, the person for whom the ampere, or amp (the unit of flow of an electrical current), was named, not only devised an international language to promote peace and unite humankind when he was eighteen years old, but also was a prolific writer regarding the philosophy of science. James Watt's ideas improved the design of the existing steam engine. An Wang invented the computer-memory core, which revolutionized the computer industry until the invention of the microchip. Biophysicist Alan Lloyd Hodgkin received a Nobel Prize for his research on nerve-cell inhibition.

Many Aquarians are interested in technology and science and have a talent for working with computers. Yours is a forward-looking, progressive sign, so you are likely to be more interested in the future than in the past. This may be why this sign has so many inventors. You have an uncanny talent for dreaming up things that people have never thought of before.

All for One and One for All

Aquarius is the sign of the humanitarian. You instinctively understand that all people are equal, that nobody is better than anybody else. All of the wars and fighting in this world mystify you. You cannot understand why people do not calmly discuss their differences and arrive at a reasonable conclusion or consensus. You are appalled by the selfishness and self-interest that you see in others. You are concerned about others' welfare. It is easy for you to be there for a friend who is going through a hard time. You will do whatever you can to help somebody, offering advice and seeking solutions. You may even be very aware of difficulties your parents are experiencing, whether they be financial or work-related. You are aware that you live in a world with other people with various problems and needs, and you have an innate desire to help.

Many Aquarians enjoy joining with others to address the injustices of the world. Aquarius Oprah Winfrey is a perfect example of an Aquarian's focus on improving people's lives. Like a contemporary Prometheus, her life is devoted to expanding people's knowledge and self-awareness. Aquarius Paul Newman was one of the first celebrities to sell consumer products, such as sauces and dressings, in order to donate the proceeds to charities. He also runs a camp for kids with cancer. Phil Collins is known for his contributions to organizations that help combat homelessness. Mia Farrow adopts children who otherwise would have a hard time finding a family. Former president Franklin D. Roosevelt instituted social programs that continue to help countless numbers of people. All of these Aquarians see other people as members of the human family and help make life better for everyone. You may be interested in volunteering for an organization whose cause is close to your heart—or even starting your own.

Cultivating a Strong Emotional Life

Part of your talent in helping people is your ability to remain detached and not become overwhelmed by your feelings.

This helps you to accomplish your goals and complete projects that others would not have the emotional stamina to undertake. But, this same gift may also inhibit your emotional life unnecessarily. You excel when it comes to rational, logical thought, but the world of the emotions is often a mystery to you. You are more comfortable thinking something through than feeling your way through a situation. You may think that emotions are illogical and unproductive. You would much rather that everybody be civil and discuss their differences calmly.

Aquarians can feel embarrassed by their feelings, as if they were not supposed to have any. You may think it is better to rise above the messiness of human emotion seeing it as something that weaker people experience. But, as an Aquarius, it is important for you to explore your feelings. Otherwise, you may decide that you don't have any emotional needs, when nothing could be further from the truth. Also, others may see you as being cold or unfeeling. For example, you may give a friend excellent advice but say it in a way that doesn't take into account your friend's feelings. When you respect your own and others' feelings, you are in touch with your extraordinary wisdom. This wisdom is the combination of the mind and heart working together.

Let others know what you need and what you feel. Although you may initially be uncomfortable in this less-familiar terrain, with practice you will be able to experience your feelings as comfortably as anyone else. Not only does cultivating a strong emotional life help nourish your spirit, but it strengthens all of your relationships as well.

Your Soul Mission: Appreciating Your Uniqueness

Sometimes you may look around and think, "What am I doing here? Who *are* these people?" Like a fish out of water, Aquarians often feel as if they do not fit in with the people around them. You may feel different from your family members, your friends, or your schoolmates. This is a normal feeling for an Aquarius and is actually a gift, although it may not always seem that way. This "differentness" is the very quality that will take you far in life. You are not here to be like everybody else. Your destiny is to be at the forefront of change, to use your brilliance to come up with something new and untested. You teach and inspire others with your unique way of looking at life. You challenge old traditions. You introduce people to ideas and experiences they haven't thought about before.

Your ruling planet, Uranus, is called the Awakener. Sometimes people need to wake up from the humdrum sameness of life and their sleepy routines. You are indeed the Awakener. Your originality is what makes people sit up and take notice of something that has never occurred to them. This is such a special destiny that it is important for you to feel good about your uniqueness.

This world is full of Aquarians who have utilized their "stranger in a strange land" experience to introduce something new to the world and help change the way people see and think. Aquarius Sarah McLachlan created Lilith Fair, an all-female concert, which proved to be enormously successful. In 1939 singer Marian Anderson was prohibited because of her race from singing in Constitution Hall in Washington, D.C. Instead, she performed for an audience of seventy-five thousand people on the steps of the Lincoln Memorial, and, by doing so, brought public awareness to existing prejudices. In testimony to a true Aquarius, Jackie Robinson's tombstone reads, "A life is not important except in the impact it has on other lives." He was the first African-American athlete to play major league baseball and the first African-American to be inducted into the Baseball Hall of Fame.

People who see a different world from what others see lead interesting lives. Your unique vision opens paths never before experienced, both for you and others. Don't make the mistake of spending your life trying to be like everybody else, or you will miss out on the exciting journey that is waiting for you.

FRIENDSHIP

Aquarians, even the ones who choose more solitary pursuits in life, love nothing better than to hang out with their friends, whether at the mall or going to the movies. Friendships are as important to you as romantic relationships. You are loyal to your friends. There is little that you would not do for them.

You love to be with people you know really well and are likely to form long-lasting friendships. You are great at giving your friends advice when they are going through difficult times. You give them something to think about that they haven't considered before. Your unusual mind and original take on life provides you with many interesting and different ideas to share with your friends.

Since you appreciate anything or anyone who is a little different, you are likely to reach out to and form friendships with people who, like you, march to the beat of a different drummer. Your friends may be from a variety of races, religions, and cultures. You appreciate individuality.

You easily bond with people who are as independent as you are and love trying out new experiences. As an air sign you are also a communicator and love nothing better than stimulating discussions with your friends.

Check out the compatibility guide later in this chapter to see how your friends' Sun signs match up with yours.

HOME LIFE

Since "Question authority" is your motto, you might not agree with all your parents' beliefs. They may have ideas about what they would like you to do, while you have completely opposite thoughts about what feels right for you. You are very much your own person. You want to be heard and you want your ideas to be respected. Since you have a highly developed concept of justice and fairness, you respond more willingly to your parents' needs when they appeal to this quality in you.

Many Aquarians feel as though they have nothing in common with their parents or other family members. You just sense that you are different in some way. For some Aquarians, their entire family is different in some way from others in the community. Whatever the source of your originality and inventiveness, your home life provides the environment for you to develop these attributes. Find a place in yourself that is okay with your differentness and learn to see it as a gift instead of a bother. You know deep in your heart that although people are quite different from one another, we are all actually part of the human family. Think of your parents as part of this larger human family, whether or not you relate to them—or they to you.

Since you love unusual things, make sure your bedroom or other areas of the house reflect your uniqueness. A painting from art class, a rare shell you found on the beach, or a book of poetry that really speaks to your heart should be out where you can enjoy them.

CAREER

Although Aquarians, like any other sign, are found in many different professions, there are particular factors to keep in mind when you are choosing a career. The first requirement is to pick one that leaves you plenty of room to express your originality. A job where you are doing the same thing day in and day out is not for you. Nor is a job where someone is breathing down your neck and telling you how to do everything! Your desire to put your own unique stamp on whatever you do needs full expression in your career. An Aquarian's independence leads some to go into business for themselves.

Aquarian artists, actors, and writers are known for their originality. They often break the rules by doing things their own way. They bring a distinctive style to their form of expression. John Belushi's comedic style was unlike anybody else's. So is Ellen Degeneres's. Chris Rock breaks all the rules with his special brand of comedy. Science-fiction writer Jules Verne wrote about the future, envisioning a world in which many of his ideas have become reality today. Cybill Shepherd is a maverick, always surprising people with what she is going to do next. John Travolta continues to amaze people with his interesting choices in acting roles.

Many Aquarians express their ideals for humanity by deciding to serve the public in some way. Towns are filled with Aquarians in political office, heading community organizations, or advocating for the rights of people. Former Aquarius presidents Abraham Lincoln, Franklin D. Roosevelt, and Ronald Reagan are all known for their unique and sometimes surprising visions for America. These are all men who marched to the beat of their own drum.

Because yours is the sign of the inventor, careers that encourage free reign for your inquiring mind are great, such as science, medicine, or any field that is involved in research. Many Aquarians have a natural ability with computers, so any job that utilizes them may attract you.

RELATIONSHIPS

A Friendship in Relationship

Your independent spirit shows up strongly in your relationships with others. You need room to breathe. You are uncompromising when it comes to your freedom. You are truly a child of the Aquarian Age, which means you want friendship in a romantic relationship. You are looking for common ground, someone with similar interests and values, someone you can actually talk to! Aquarians often choose their relationships using the same criteria they use for choosing friends. You may even find a close friendship turning into a romantic relationship.

Because you are very much your own person and do not like anyone telling you what to do, you will need to watch out for being stubborn and uncompromising in your relationships. You like to maintain control and may mistakenly interpret perfectly reasonable requests from the person you care for as threats to your freedom.

How close is too close? For you, as an Aquarius, balancing your desire for closeness with your desire for freedom is your relationship theme. You will need to remind yourself that it really is okay to open your heart to someone, to show that you care. You hate jealousy and some of the silly dramatic displays you see others play out in their relationships. And as much as you want to throw yourself wholeheartedly into your relationship, you also want to play it cool and protect yourself from being struck by Cupid's arrow.

The fact is, there is nothing like being in love and opening your heart to soften the effects of your rational mind. Love opens up emotions you never knew existed. To enjoy the incredible feeling when your heart opens up to someone, try to resist the impulse to logically categorize your emotions. Have fun being romantic. Although it's like being on a roller-coaster ride at times, it is also one of the most magical states you will ever experience. Enjoy it!

Sign Compatibility

There are some basic concepts to keep in mind when you are thinking about compatibility. You want to remember that although Sun sign characteristics describe central and important themes in life, the Sun does not represent the *whole* person. Planets, particularly Venus, are also important to consider when determining compatibility between people. Venus is the planet that symbolizes your concept of an ideal relationship. It describes how you like to give and receive affection. The sign that Venus occupied at the time of your birth explains what is most important to you when you are in love. Other planets are equally important when it comes to relationships: Mercury is the planet that reveals your communication style; Mars is the planet of action and desire. The Moon shows your emotional temperament and security concerns.

Signs that are opposite each other in the zodiac are often compatible, although their personality characteristics are very different. Leo is Aquarius's opposite sign.

Now, with these considerations in place, we can proceed!

COMPATIBILITY GUIDE

Aquarius and Aries

You appreciate an Aries' independent, fiery, and pioneering spirit. An Aries loves your unconventional approach to life and your freedom-loving ways. You both need room to breathe and won't try to hold on too tightly to the other.

The challenge: Both independent people, your travels may eventually take you in different directions if you don't make a point to travel together.

Aquarius and Taurus

You are both strong, determined people who know how to stand your ground. You appreciate a Taurus's loyalty and are intrigued by his or her earthy, stable personality. You spice up your Taurus's life by thinking up new and interesting things to do and places to go.

The challenge: A Taurus is more conservative than you are and may be wary of your unconventional ways. You will both have to appreciate the differences in your personalities for this relationship to feel comfortable.

Aquarius and Gemini

Both air signs, the two of you will never run out of things to talk about. You love a Gemini's interesting mind. Your independent, do-your-own-thing vibe is attractive to a Gemini. The two of you instinctively understand each other. Life is fun when you are together.

The challenge: There is such a thing as too much talk and not enough action! You two will need to make sure that you do things as well as talk about them to keep this relationship on a forward track.

Aquarius and Cancer

You are both compassionate people, although you have significantly different ways of looking at and experiencing life. You are independent and need plenty of room to breathe. A Cancer seeks emotional connection and likes to be close and involved.

The challenge: As an air sign, you can be detached and logical. Cancer, a water sign, is very much into feelings. You will need to be sensitive to your Cancer's emotional comfort for this relationship to flourish.

Aquarius and Leo

Leo is your opposite sign, and, since opposites attract, this creates compatibility. You are drawn to a Leo's strength, loyalty, and warmth. A Leo appreciates your independence and originality. The differences in your temperaments naturally complement each other.

The challenge: You both are strong, determined, and like to get your own way. Flexibility is the key to making this relationship work.

Aquarius and Virgo

Both of you have high standards, although your definition of them may differ. You love Virgo's practicality and earthy sensibility. Your Virgo appreciates your unusual mind. The two of you find plenty to talk about and plenty of interesting things to do.

The challenge: Because Virgos tend to be more reserved than you are, your color-outside-of-the-lines personality can be unnerving. Be sensitive to these differences in your personalities to help this relationship thrive.

Aquarius and Libra

With a Libra you will never be at a loss for something to talk about. You share the air element and love to use your minds, discuss issues, and plan for the future. You both have a keen sense of justice and fairness and find it easy to relate to each other.

The challenge: Libras love to be close and spend lots of time together. You like to devote plenty of time to hanging out with your friends. Be supportive of each other's needs to help this relationship grow.

Aquarius and Scorpio

You are both strong, interesting, and determined people. Scorpios respond to the world through their feelings; your style is to be emotionally detached and logical. The differences between you are what you find attractive in this relationship.

The challenge: You will need to be comfortable with your Scorpio's intense emotional life and more reserved nature to be happy in this relationship.

Aquarius and Sagittarius

You are both freedom-loving, independent people, so neither one of you will try to hold the other one back. Life is exciting and fun and often an adventure with your Sagittarius. You will find plenty of interesting activities to please you both.

The challenge: You love to discuss the pros and cons of any situation; Sagittarians like to be on the go and are generally less communicative than you are. Keep your traveling shoes close by to keep this relationship on track.

Aquarius and Capricorn

A Capricorn's down-to-earth personality attracts you, while your quirky independence is intriguing to a Capricorn. While you love to break all the rules, a Capricorn tends to be reserved and cautious. These different approaches to life can be what keep this relationship so interesting.

The challenge: Your independent style may be a lot for your Capricorn to handle at times. Be sensitive to your Capricorn's more reserved manner to help this relationship last.

Aquarius and Aquarius

You are two independent free thinkers. Comfortable in the air element, you find plenty to talk about to keep you interested in each other. A good friendship is important to both of you. Neither of you tries to hold the other back.

The challenge: You both love your independence so much that your interests may take you in entirely different directions. You'll have to make a point of spending plenty of time together to keep your bond close.

Aquarius and Pisces

Although your personalities are quite different, you both are dreamers at heart, which helps to create a lasting bond. You admire and relate to the lack of selfishness in your Pisces. A Pisces is attracted to your innovative and unusual take on life.

The challenge: Pisceans are in tune with their feelings, while you tend to be more detached. Be sensitive and understanding of this difference to help this relationship feel comfortable.

SPECIAL TIPS FOR AQUARIANS

Below are reminders and special tips that will help any Aquarius lead a successful and fulfilling life. Maximize your positive traits, and be aware of those traits that can hold you back. Make the effort to learn from your mistakes, and keep your eyes on the stars!

1. March to the beat of your own drum.
2. Stay in touch with your feelings.
3. Celebrate your uniqueness.
4. Get involved in humanitarian causes.
5. Be purposeful rather than simply rebellious.
6. Honor your independence without separating yourself from others.
7. Let people know what you need, what is important to you.
8. Stay tuned into your wisdom.
9. Be sensitive to others' feelings.
10. Find the balance between freedom and closeness.

You, dear Aquarius, are an independent free spirit. The incredible gift of originality and your unusual, brilliant mind need to be honored and utilized. March to the beat of your own drum, and you will create an exceptional, remarkable life.

Pisces

The Dream Seeker
February 19 to March 20

Symbol: The Fish
Ruling planet: Neptune
Element: Water—*sensitive, intuitive, feels deeply*
Mode: Mutable—*adaptable, changeable, restless*
Birthstone: Aquamarine
Color: Sea green

FAMOUS PISCES PEOPLE:

February 19	Prince Andrew	February 25	Pierre-Auguste Renoir
February 20	Cindy Crawford		
February 21	Jennifer Love Hewitt	February 26	Erykah Badu
		February 27	Chelsea Clinton
February 22	Drew Barrymore	February 28	Linus Pauling
February 23	W. E. B. DuBois	February 29	Ann Lee
February 24	Edward James Olmos	March 1	Ron Howard
		March 2	Jon Bon Jovi

March 3	Alexander Graham Bell	March 12	James Taylor
March 4	Mirium Makeba	March 13	Percival Lowell
March 5	Niki Taylor	March 14	Albert Einstein
March 6	Shaquille O'Neal	March 15	Michelangelo
March 7	Piet Mondrian	March 16	Jerry Lewis
March 8	Freddie Prinze Jr.	March 17	Gary Sinise
March 9	James Van Der Beek	March 18	Queen Latifah
March 10	Sharon Stone	March 19	Bruce Willis
March 11	Alex Kingston	March 20	Spike Lee

THESE BEHAVIORS AND ATTITUDES INCREASE CONFIDENCE

Empathy
Kindness
Gentleness
Affection
Sensitivity
Giving
Imagination

THESE BEHAVIORS AND ATTITUDES DECREASE CONFIDENCE

Indiscrimination
Unreliability
Gullibility
Impracticality
Evasiveness
Undisciplined tendency
Inconsistency

THE DREAM SEEKER

If you can imagine it, you can make it real. This could very well be the motto for every Pisces. Your sign is filled with some of the most visionary, brilliant, and imaginative people this world has ever seen. Pisces are the dream seekers of the zodiac, whose ideals have contributed to making this world more beautiful, more compassionate, and infinitely more interesting. You are an idealist at heart, and, at your best, nothing holds you back from fulfilling your dreams.

Pisces Albert Einstein, one of the world's greatest thinkers, envisioned completely new ways of understanding the universe. George Washington, the first president of the United States, had a dream that thirteen English colonies could be transformed into a self-governing nation. Michelangelo's imagination produced some of the world's most magnificent art, and Elizabeth Barrett Browning's some of the most beautiful poetry.

Many artists, actors, and musicians populate this creative sign. Jennifer Love Hewitt, Drew Barrymore, Camryn Manheim, Edward James Olmos, Holly Hunter, Freddie Prinze Jr., and James Van Der Beek are just a few of the many Pisces actors who bring their talents to television and film. Pisces musicians and songwriters include George Harrison, Kurt Cobain, Jon Bon Jovi, and Erykah Badu. Painters Pierre-Auguste Renoir and Piet Mondrian were Pisces. Ralph Ellison, Jack Kerouac, Anaïs Nin, and Theodor Geisel (Dr. Seuss) were Piscean writers. The sports world has also had its share of Pisces, including basketball greats Shaquille O'Neal and Julius Erving, and track-and-field dynamo Jackie Joyner-Kersee.

All of these Pisces allowed their dreams, ideals, and imagination to motivate them to create interesting, fulfilling lives. By staying in touch with your dreams, you, too, can design an exciting, rewarding life. Your rich imagination provides you with one of the gifts of your sign: your ability to engage the world of make-believe. Some people become cynical as they grow older, but you know how to keep your dreams alive. Make sure you give your imagination a focus. Many Pisces blossom when they have a creative outlet. Art, music, or dance classes can provide this. If you are a writer, write in your journal or enter a poetry contest. Bring your creativity and your brilliance into this world by cultivating focus and discipline. Your talent for seeing the magic in life is like a guiding star, which can lead you toward the fulfillment of your dreams. The mythologist Joseph Campbell said, "Follow your bliss," which means do what your heart tells you to do. Do what sparks your passion. To make a dream come true, give it a direction; to make your dream come true, follow your heart.

Keep Your Head in the Stars and Your Feet on the Ground

Pisces' symbol portrays two fish swimming in opposite directions. In the constellation, the southern fish and the northern fish are connected by a single star. One fish represents the body and the material world, and the other the soul or spiritual world. A Pisces' life journey is about learning how to balance both worlds. Combining them by manifesting your soul's longing on Earth is one of the highest expressions of your sign.

Some ancient cultures chose the dolphin to symbolize Pisces. The dolphin is seen as gentle and is known to save people who are lost at sea. The dolphin is a fitting symbol for you. You are sensitive to the sorrows in this world, and helping and even rescuing people from hardship is one of your strongest drives.

Bringing Your Dreams into the World

Because the dream world is so attractive, there are times when you may be reluctant to come back to ordinary life and reality. But, turning away from the sometimes harsh realities of earthly living prohibits you from manifesting your dreams and also robs humanity of your incredible talents. It is a gift that you can enter into the magic realms where many others cannot go. What you *do* with what you experience is what matters. Don't become disillusioned by the problems of the world; instead create a better world.

Pisceans need to have something to devote themselves to, to have something to believe in. Think about what is important to you. What is your passion? Where do your desires lead you? You are blessed with the gift of imagination and an idealistic nature. Give yourself a goal, a guiding star to follow.

One way to help you channel your imagination is to pay attention to your dreams. The Native Americans created something called a dream catcher. These beautifully woven objects often decorated with feathers and beads are placed above the bed. The idea is that when you go to sleep and dream, this dream catcher will help keep your dreams with you in waking life. Placing a dream catcher near your bed stimulates you to remember and then manifest your dreams.

Living in both the dream world and the material world can be confusing. It may be difficult for you to shake off your daydreams and come back to Earth. Teachers or others may say to you, "Pay attention!" The fact is, paying attention to the details and some of the more practical concerns of earthly living may not come easily to you. Learning to keep a foot in this world without losing the magic of the dream world is one of your most important lessons in life. If you remain in the dream world too long, it may be difficult to find your way back. If you ignore your dreams and try to be really practical, you will feel like you are missing out on something important. All Pisceans need to be involved in activities that give room for both worlds.

A Compassionate Heart

You yearn for a better world. Many Pisces devote themselves to improving the world by getting involved in organizations where they can help others. Pisces Ralph Nader's concern for public safety prompted him to become a consumer-rights advocate to protect people from unscrupulous business practices and dangerous products. Pisces Ralph Abernathy, a civil-rights activist, cofounded (along with Martin Luther King, Jr.) the Southern Christian Leadership Conference, an organization dedicated to coordinating the activities of civil-rights groups. Alexander Graham Bell, although famous for inventing the telephone, devoted his life to his passion for teaching the deaf to speak. In fact, he used the money awarded to him for his telephone invention to establish an international information center for the education of the deaf. The writer Victor Hugo wrote novels that highlighted political and social injustices, including *Les Misérables* and *The Hunchback of Notre Dame*. Elizabeth Taylor is credited for bringing attention to the plight of people suffering from AIDS and has raised millions of dollars for AIDS research.

These people are typical generous, caring, and empathic Pisceans. You are especially sensitive to the feelings of the disadvantaged, the underdog, and basically anyone or anything that needs help. You are likely to take home a stray cat, to rescue a hurt bird, and to befriend people whom others ignore. You are strongly connected to and aware of the larger world.

Who Am I and What Am I Doing Here?

Many Pisces feel different from other people. The things that worry others often don't bother you at all. You find it difficult to understand why people fight and argue about things that make absolutely no sense to you. People's priorities can seem backward. For example, people may be worried about being in the "right crowd" but not as concerned with the real problems of the world. As far as you are concerned, people worry about the wrong things. Sometimes you may feel as if you were dropped onto the earth from another planet. In many ways, you are a child of the cosmos even though your feet are planted here on Earth.

Although you feel different, paradoxically, it is easy for you to relate to many different kinds of people. Partly this is because you don't place people in separate categories. You instinctively know that we are all part of the same universe, that we are all connected. However, if you don't gain emotional distance, others' problems can seem overwhelming. If you are around people who are sad or angry, you may absorb their feelings and end up feeling sad and angry. Make sure that you spend time alone to center yourself. If you are around people who are angry, go to another room or go outside and walk around the block. Remove yourself from stressful environments whenever possible. All Pisces need a special place to be alone. All Pisces need a sanctuary.

The Chameleon

The ability to relate to so many different kinds of people may make you wonder, "If I can be all of these different ways with all of these different people, then who am I?" Your sensitivity and empathy make it easy for you to identify with others and also allow people to see themselves in you. This is a gift that will help you in your life, but it also requires that you are as clear as possible about your own values and about what is important to you. Otherwise, you may find yourself living out somebody else's dream or fulfilling someone else's needs that have nothing to do with your own. Trust your intuition, and listen to guidance from within to be clear about what feels right for you.

Searching for Paradise on Earth

To allow your idealism to work positively for you, watch out for the tendency to put on rose-colored glasses, which means seeing only what you want to see. For example, you may decide that someone is telling you the truth when common sense would tell you otherwise. Pisceans sometimes think, "If I pretend it's not happening, then it isn't." Or you may insist on noticing only the good qualities about someone, while ignoring the destructive behaviors. The fact is, you have an incredible ability to see the beauty and goodness in people; you see straight through to their souls. The problem is that seeing only the potential of someone and not the reality of what they are doing right now does not give you the whole picture. Pisces people can create problems for themselves by this peculiar insistence on refusing to recognize the reality of certain situations.

Riding the Waves

Pisces is one of the most sensitive signs of the zodiac. No one needs to take a heavy-handed approach with you. Your feelings are so near the surface and you have such a psychic attunement to your environment that when you do something you know you shouldn't have done, you already feel bad enough about it! You respond to the world through your feelings, which are like an inner-guidance system for you.

Because your sensitivity is one of your greatest gifts, value and utilize your sensitivity rather than try to hide it. What do your feelings motivate you to do? They need to be channeled; they need a focus. Otherwise you may be flooded by your emotions, needs, and desires and feel unable to do anything with them. Think of the ocean as a big pool of feelings, creativity, and imagination. You can just drift in the ocean, swimming aimlessly and allowing the currents to take you to and fro. Or, you can be a surfer riding the waves. Following each wave all the way out is not only fun, but also when the wave goes back into the ocean, it replenishes and renews itself, producing another wave. You, too, will feel energized and renewed if you keep going back to your source, your inner self or spiritual center. Trust the waves, ride with them, and have fun playing with them. The ocean is like your creative source. The waves are your creativity manifested.

Sacrifice

The term *sacrifice* means different things to different people: "to give up something now for gain in the future"; "to put someone else's needs before one's own"; or "to give up something that is valued." However this term is defined, Pisces people often do not think of sacrifice in the same way that others do. You instinctively think of others as much as you think of yourself. For example, you may not feel that helping out on a weekend to feed homeless people is a sacrifice. It's just something you want to do. On the other hand, you may feel guilty if you don't put your own needs aside for others. It is important to find the balance between doing for others and doing for yourself.

Many people are not willing to make the necessary sacrifices to manifest their dreams. You have a special ability to make sacrifices when required. Again, making a sacrifice to help you attain your own goals is as important as making a sacrifice to help someone else.

Giving and Receiving

You are a generous person. The act of giving is second nature to you. The act of receiving may be more difficult, although allowing others to do something for you is just as important. When you receive from others, whether it is a gift, a compliment, or help with something, your relationships are brought into balance. At times you may focus so much on meeting other people's needs that you forget about your own or feel that your own needs are less important. Perhaps you think that if you don't do what others want you to do, they won't like you or want to be with you. Maybe you feel selfish or guilty for having needs or wanting to do something just for yourself.

If people want to do something for you, do you tell them not to bother? When someone compliments you, do you brush it off as unimportant? The act of receiving means accepting graciously and gratefully all of the wonderful words, compliments, gifts, and offers of assistance that come your way. Simply saying thank you with a smile lets people know that you have received what has been given to you with pleasure. When people are ready to receive, life sends them people who are willing to give.

If you feel as if a relationship is mostly about the other person's needs or that you are being taken advantage of, ask yourself, "Am I willing to receive from this person?" If you do not make your needs important, others may not, either. Make sure *you* give to you, and others will also. Finding the balance between giving and receiving and learning to balance your own needs with others' needs is part of every Pisces' path.

Your Soul Mission: Cultivating Consistency

Part of being a dream seeker is to give yourself the room to make changes as your dreams change. You may take a dance class one year and an art class the next. Your adaptable nature makes it easy to express your creativity in a variety of ways. Because of this, you may explore so many things at once that you don't fully develop any one talent. Take the time to completely delve into the subject that interests you. If you reach for a star to which you have not built a ladder, you may become disillusioned when you do not reach your goal.

Developing consistency and reliability is one of every Pisces' greatest tasks. Your dreams and goals will require effort and hard work to achieve. If you stay in the world of fantasy, playing in your mind all of the great things you could do and be, then your dreams will not materialize. It is necessary to trade the fantasy for the dream. An active, rich fantasy life is both a blessing and a curse. If it becomes a place of refuge to run away from hardships in life, then you won't be able make your dreams come true. If you use it as a launching pad, there is nothing in this world that is not yours for the taking.

Build a strong foundation for your dreams by taking the concrete steps to build that stairway to the stars. Don't just think you would like to write a poem—write it. Don't just daydream about making a new friend—reach out to people. Don't just fantasize about doing better in school—study. Don't just want to play piano well—practice. Making your dreams come true is always within your reach. Build the foundation by developing consistency.

FRIENDSHIP

Your friends benefit greatly from your kindness. You are compassionate and sympathetic to your friends' problems. If they need a shoulder to cry on, you are available. You have a special cosmic wisdom, which makes you great at telling them what is worth worrying about and what to let go of.

Pisceans are often shy, so getting to know someone takes time. You are not an open book and need to feel your way into a friendship to be sure that it is right for you. Once you get to know people, you are much more relaxed and comfortable.

Receiving as well as giving is important in all your relationships, including your friendships. Don't limit yourself to just having friends who pour their problems out to you. Let your friends know what is going on with you, and give them the opportunity to support you. That way your friends will not drain you. They will be fun to be with.

You, more than any other sign in the zodiac, are likely to form friendships with people whom others pass by. Since you have a special knack for being able to see the beauty and goodness in everyone, you are willing to give people a chance. This quality will always give you more friends than you can count.

Check out the compatibility guide later in this chapter to see how your friends' Sun signs match up with yours.

HOME LIFE

Your sensitive nature makes you an emotional barometer for your family. You feel what they are feeling whether or not family members talk freely about their emotions. You soak up the vibes in the household. With your uncanny psychic attunement, you probably don't even have to be in the same room your mother is in to know whether she is happy or sad.

A variety of Piscean themes may show up in your family life. You may see someone making sacrifices, introducing you to the theme of giving and receiving. Perhaps a family member is artistic or imaginative. The importance of creating a spiritual life may be a key value. You may even have a relative who has psychic abilities. Cultivate and express your most positive Piscean qualities within your family environment.

Make sure you have a quiet place to go to be alone. You need a peaceful, quiet, soothing environment whenever possible. You may want to place a dream catcher by your bed along with pictures of fish or dolphins. Make sure you have meaningful belongings close by: a journal with your poetry, your favorite CDs, or your drawings and paintings.

CAREER

It is important for every Pisces to have something to believe in, to have a passion for, and something to which they can dedicate themselves. Although Pisces are in many different professions and defy any strict classification, at the heart of every Pisces is someone who dreams big and has great potential to achieve whatever the imagination can produce. Consistency and taking the necessary steps will be the keys to career fulfillment.

A quiet and peaceful work environment is best for you. Noisy, rambunctious, or chaotic working conditions could feel stressful. In general, jobs that establish clear guidelines and provide a structure are helpful to you.

Many Pisces are drawn to the helping professions. The world is filled with Pisces nurses, doctors, social workers, psychologists, healers, and religious leaders. Professions where you can make a difference in people's lives allow your idealism full expression. Even if helping others does not become your career, you are still likely to help someone or some organization. Pisces Jerry Lewis has become as famous for his yearly telethons for muscular dystrophy as for his comedy and acting.

There are plenty of Pisces musicians, painters, actors, and artists of all kinds, many who were mentioned earlier in the chapter. Even if art is not a career choice, many Pisces choose to make time to paint, draw, sing, or play an instrument.

RELATIONSHIPS

Seeking a Soul Connection

Pisces Elizabeth Barrett Browning began her famous poem, "How do I love thee? Let me count the ways. . . ." Ahhh, the romance! The poetry! You are romantic to your core, and nothing captures your heart as much as the gentle words of love.

More than anything, you are looking to make a spiritual connection, to find someone with whom you can share your dreams. Neptune, your ruling planet, represents spiritual love. The desire to experience this deeper connection is at the center of your relationship longings.

A loving and kind person, you would do almost anything for someone you love. You are giving; you like to meet others' needs; and you hate to disappoint people. Probably a little shy, you are likely to take your time getting to know someone. Although you may feel the magic right away, you know that love takes time to deepen and that with time love becomes even more powerful.

You respond to the world through your feelings, and nowhere is this more apparent than in your relationships. You lead with your heart, not with your head, because your heart shows you the soul of a person. Here, as in other areas of your life, you see the beauty that others do not notice. It is important for you to think through your attractions, since you are more adept at seeing the soul than the mortal human being. You may idealize the person you care for, putting him

or her on a pedestal. Your facility with the dream world and
your fantasies may cloud over good judgment when it comes
to your relationship choices. Make sure you do not have on
rose-colored glasses, or you could fall in love with a fantasy
instead of a real person.

Your impulse to rescue people can cause you to be
attracted to those with a lot of problems. There is nothing
wrong with helping others, but make sure you stay tuned
into your own needs so that the relationship has give-and-
take. The give-and-take is what establishes the spiritual connection. Doing all of the giving while the other person does
all of the taking not only prevents the spiritual connection
you are seeking, but over time it will also make you angry
and resentful. Pay attention to your own needs, and always
honor what feels right for you.

Sign Compatibility

There are some basic concepts to keep in mind when you are
thinking about compatibility. You want to remember that
although Sun sign characteristics describe central and important themes in life, the Sun does not represent the *whole* person. Planets, particularly Venus, are also important to consider
when determining compatibility between people. Venus is the
planet that symbolizes your concept of an ideal relationship. It
describes how you like to give and receive affection. The sign
that Venus occupied at the time of your birth explains what is
most important to you when you are in love. Other planets are
equally important when it comes to relationships: Mercury is
the planet that reveals your communication style; Mars is the
planet of action and desire. The Moon shows your emotional
temperament and security concerns.

Signs that are opposite each other in the zodiac are often
compatible, although their personality characteristics are
very different. Virgo is Pisces' opposite sign.

Now, with these considerations in place, we can proceed!

COMPATIBILITY GUIDE

Pisces and Aries

You are both idealistic, although you respond to the world in significantly different ways. You are intrigued by the gutsy, can-do attitude of an Aries, and an Aries is fascinated by your gentle, kind personality. Never boring, this relationship allows you to have a great time romancing life and each other.

The challenge: This water/fire combination can either steam things up or burn you out. Leave plenty of room for your Aries' independent nature for this relationship to work.

Pisces and Taurus

Two gentle souls come together to create magic. You are both affectionate and find it is easy to express your devotion to each other. A Taurus helps you keep your feet on the ground and loves helping you make your dreams a reality.

The challenge: A Taurus tends to be more practical than you are. For this relationship to flourish, allow this different approach to life help you build a strong foundation for your dreams.

Pisces and Gemini

You are both imaginative people, which connects the two of you in a unique way. You are enchanted by your Gemini's mischievous and playful nature, while you bring the world of feelings and a special kind of poetry into his or her life.

The challenge: The difference in your personalities can be attractive. However, Geminis love to chat, so strengthen your communication skills to keep this relationship on track.

Pisces and Cancer

You two can be positively psychic with each other! Naturally affectionate, romantic, and sensitive to each other's feelings, it is easy for you to create a lasting bond. Your Cancer is very protective of you and will work overtime to make sure you are comfortable.

The challenge: Both water signs, you may become overly "touchy" or moody. Communicate your feelings rather than assuming your Cancer knows what is going on with you. Honest communication deepens this relationship.

Pisces and Leo

A Leo's fun, playful nature and sense of drama brings a ray of sunshine into your life. Leos are attracted to your sensitivity and your gentle, soothing touch. Although you have different approaches to life, you are both idealistic and can be great supporters of each other's dreams.

The challenge: You tend to be flexible, while Leos can be stubborn. Your Leo needs to respect your feelings, while you need to accommodate your Leo's love of being in charge for this relationship to work.

Pisces and Virgo

Virgo is your opposite sign, which forms a natural attraction. You love the can-do personality of a Virgo. Your Virgo is attracted to your imaginative, dreamy nature. You both love to do things for each other and find it easy to tune into each other's needs and desires.

The challenge: A Virgo has a wonderful commonsense approach to the world; you rely on feelings and faith. Appreciating what each of you has to offer brings balance into this relationship.

Pisces and Libra

You are both natural-born romantics who know how to tune into each other's mind, heart, and soul. Neither of you wants to make waves; you would rather accommodate the other's needs. In this relationship, it feels natural and easy to support each other.

The challenge: While you both naturally focus on the other's needs and happiness, make sure you let your Libra know what is important to you, and encourage your Libra to do the same to help this relationship thrive.

Pisces and Scorpio

Both water signs, your sensitivity helps you instinctively understand each other. Your Scorpio is drawn to your kindness and your compassion. You are intrigued by the depth and intensity of your Scorpio. You find a kindred spirit in each other.

The challenge: When two water signs are together, it is necessary at times to come up for air! Although both of you like to spend time together, make sure you also get out and spend time with friends to avoid claustrophobia in this relationship.

Pisces and Sagittarius

You find a Sagittarian's outgoing, charming personality attractive. A Sagittarius is easily drawn to your compassionate heart. You are both dreamers and idealists, which can create a strong bond. It is the difference in your personalities that can be fascinating in this relationship.

The challenge: Sagittarius is a freedom-loving sign and needs plenty of room. You prefer more together time. Leave plenty of space for your Sagittarian's need to explore for this relationship to work.

Pisces and Capricorn

The practicality and ambitiousness of a Capricorn is attractive to you. A Capricorn loves your imaginative, dreamy nature. This water/earth combination brings together two kindred souls. You love being with someone who knows how to be in this world, and your Capricorn finds your cosmic consciousness irresistible.

The challenge: You tend to be more easygoing than a Capricorn, who is often looking for a mountain to climb. Learn to be comfortable with and supportive of your Capricorn's ambitious personality for this relationship to flourish.

Pisces and Aquarius
Although your personalities are quite different, you are both dreamers at heart and have a unique and innovative take on life. You love the independent do-your-own-thing style of your Aquarius, while your Aquarius admires your sensitivity and your lack of selfishness.

The challenge: You are content to spend time alone with just each other, while your Aquarius loves to hang out with friends. Support your Aquarian's friendship focus to help this relationship grow.

Pisces and Pisces
The two of you are so tuned into each other that you probably can relate telepathically! You easily identify with each other, making it easy to both give and receive support. Imaginative, creative, and somewhat otherworldly, you totally understand each other's heart.

The challenge: Since both of you can step into the dream world at will, make sure that one of you has a foot on the earth plane so you don't get lost in the stars.

SPECIAL TIPS FOR PISCES

Below are reminders and special tips that will help any Pisces lead a successful and fulfilling life. Maximize your positive traits, and be aware of those traits that can hold you back. Make the effort to learn from your mistakes, and keep your eyes on the stars!

1. Pursue your dreams. Ride the waves.
2. Give your imagination a focus, a guiding star to follow.
3. Do not put on rose-colored glasses. Go for the dream, not the fantasy.
4. Give to yourself; receive from others.
5. Don't become disillusioned by the problems of the world. Create a better world.
6. Your sensitivity is one of your greatest gifts. Don't hide it!
7. Create a sanctuary, a peaceful place where you can be alone.
8. Keep your head in the stars and your feet on the ground.
9. Develop consistency. Follow through on your ideas and ideals.
10. Find a creative outlet.

You, dear Pisces, are the dream seeker of the zodiac. Your dreams will take you as far as you want to go if you keep your feet on the ground. Remember: *If you can imagine it, you can make it real*. Manifest your heart's desire and you will lead a fulfilling life.

*

Resources

How to Find Your Time of Birth
To obtain a copy of your birth chart (also called natal chart), which is a map of the sky at the time you were born, you need to know your time of birth as well as your date and place of birth. It is especially important to know your time of birth if you were born on the cusp of a sign. For example, if you were born on March 21, you will not know if you have a Pisces or Aries Sun sign without knowing the time of your birth.

There are a few places you can look to find your time of birth:

* Ask your parents if they have a copy of the hospital birth record. This is the document that has all of the information about your birth: how much you weighed, the time and date of your birth, your parents' names, etc.
* If your parents do not have the hospital record, they may have recorded your birth time in a baby book.
* Your parents may have a copy of your birth certificate. Some states, territories, and countries list the time of birth on the birth certificate.
* Your parents may remember what time you were born. The more correct the time, the more accurate the birth chart will be. So it is important to know a specific time rather than, for example, knowing you were born around four P.M.

✳ If you cannot find your hospital record, your birth certificate, or information from a baby book, you can order your birth certificate or hospital record from the Bureau of Vital Statistics, which is located in each state's capital in the United States. Some states list the time of birth on the birth certificate. For others you will need to request the hospital birth record. Other countries also have a government office where birth records are kept. Hospitals generally do not keep birth records.

For a small fee, you can order *Where to Write for Vital Records,* which is published by the U.S. Department of Health and Human Services. It lists the addresses for all states in the United States as well as for American Samoa, the Canal Zone, the District of Columbia, Guam, the Mariana Islands, Puerto Rico, Saipon, and the Virgin Islands.
    Write to:

Superintendent of Documents
U.S. Government Printing Office
Washinton, D.C. 20402

Or, go to http://www.vitalrec.com to find the address for all states, territories, and countries. When ordering a birth certificate or hospital birth record from a government office, it is important to specifically request the time of birth.
    There is a fee to order a birth certificate or record, the amount of which varies depending upon the state, territory, or country.

How to Obtain Your Astrology Birth Chart

You can get a copy of your birth chart for a small fee or at no cost from the following companies, all of which offer a variety of astrological services. You will need to provide your date, time, and place of birth.

Astro Communication Services, Inc.
5521 Ruffin Road
San Diego, CA 92123
1-800-888-9983
Web site: http://www.astrocom.com

Astrolabe
P.O. Box 1750
Brewster, MA 02631
1-800-843-6682
Web site: http://www.alabe.com

Astrological Services
Amanda Owen
P.O. Box 502
Lansdowne, PA 19050
E-mail: amanda@AmandaOwen.com
Web sites:
http://www.AmandaOwen.com and
http://www.AstrologyForTeens.com

Astrodienst
http://www.astrodienst.com

Zodiacal Zephyr
http://www.zodiacal.com

Astrology Organizations
American Federation of Astrologers (AFA)
P.O. Box 22040
Tempe, AZ 85285-2040
888-301-7630
Web site: http://www.astrologers.com

Association for Astrological Networking (AFAN)
8306 Wilshire Blvd., PMB 537
Beverly Hills, CA 90211
Web site: http://www.afan.org

International Society for Astrological Research (ISAR)
P.O. Box 38613
Los Angeles, CA 90038-0613
815-525-0461
Web site: http://www.isarastrology.com

National Council for Geocosmic Research (NCGR)
P.O. Box 38866
Los Angeles, CA 90038
Web site: http://www.geocosmic.org

The Astrological Association of Great Britain (AA)
Unit 168, Lee Valley Technopark
Tottenham Hale, London N179LN UK
0181-880-4848
Web site: http://www.astrologer.com

Astrology Magazines
The Mountain Astrologer
P.O. Box 790
Cedar Ridge, CA 95924
800-287-4828
Web site: http://www.MountainAstrologer.com

Dell Horoscope
For subscription information:
1-800-888-6901

American Astrology
For subscription information:
American Astrology, Dept. 4
P.O. Box 2021
Marion, OH 43305-2021

Go to www.AmandaOwen.com or www.AstrologyForTeens.
com for information and links to a variety of astrological resources including:

* Sun sign descriptions
* Weekly horoscopes
* Celebrity birth dates
* Questions about your own birth chart
* Astrology organizations
* Astrological publications

You can learn more about the people mentioned in
this book by going to http://www.britannica.com or www.
celebsite.com.

Famous Sun Signs

MORE FAMOUS ARIES

Jane Goodall	April 3
David Letterman	April 12
Sandra Day O'Connor	March 26
Colin Powell	April 5
William Shatner	March 22
Gloria Steinem	March 25
Quentin Tarantino	March 27
Bob Woodward	March 26

MORE FAMOUS TAUREANS

Richard Avedon	May 15
Annette Bening	May 29
Willem de Kooning	April 24
Wayne Dyer	May 10
Martha Graham	May 11
Jay Leno	April 28
Shirley MacLaine	April 24
Florence Nightingale	May 12
Al Pacino	April 25
Dennis Rodman	May 13
Oskar Schindler	April 28
Pyotr Ilich Tchaikovsky	May 7
Stevie Wonder	May 13

MORE FAMOUS GEMINIS

Tim Allen	June 13
Margaret Bourke-White	June 14
James Brown	June 17
Drew Carey	May 23
Mary Cassatt	May 22
Gail Godwin	June 18
Lillian Hellman	June 20
Joe Piscopo	June 17
Maurice Sendak	June 10
John Wesley	June 17

MORE FAMOUS CANCERS

Arthur Ashe	July 10
Pearl Buck	June 26
Tom Hanks	July 9
Beck (Hansen)	July 8
George Orwell	June 25
Princess Diana	July 1
Della Reese	July 6
Henry David Thoreau	July 12
Suzanne Vega	July 11

MORE FAMOUS LEOS

Angela Bassett	August 16
Alexander Fleming	August 6
Henry Ford	July 30
Mick Jagger	July 26
Julie Krone	July 24
Stanley Kubrick	July 26

Jennifer Lopez	July 24
Sean Penn	August 17
J. K. Rowling	July 31
Arnold Schwarzenegger	July 30
Hilary Swank	July 30

MORE FAMOUS VIRGOS

Jane Addams	September 6
Ingrid Bergman	August 28
Sean Connery	August 25
David Copperfield	September 16
Elvis Costello	August 25
Jane Curtin	September 6
Lee De Forest	August 26
Scott Hamilton	August 28
Michael Jackson	August 28
Tommy Lee Jones	September 15
John Locke	August 29
Marlee Matlin	August 24
Maria Montessori	August 31
Van Morrison	August 31
Bill Murray	September 21
Arnold Palmer	September 10
J. C. Penney	September 16
Regis Philbin	August 25
Walter Reed	September 13
LeAnn Rimes	August 28
Harland "Colonel" Sanders	September 9
Upton Sinclair	September 20
Leo Tolstoy	September 9
Lily Tomlin	September 1

MORE FAMOUS LIBRAS

Jimmy Carter	October 1
Bob Geldof	October 5
Václav Havel	October 5
William Penn	October 14
Desmond Tutu	October 7

MORE FAMOUS SCORPIOS

F. Murray Abraham	October 24
Christiaan Barnard	November 8
Fyodor Dostoyevsky	November 11
Richard Dreyfuss	October 29
Gertrude Ederle	October 23
Sally Field	November 6
Calista Flockhart	November 11
William Herschel	November 15
Soichiro Honda	November 17
Demi Moore	November 11
Julia Roberts	October 28
Auguste Rodin	November 12
Florence Sabin	November 9
Carl Sagan	November 9
Jonas Edward Salk	October 28
Robert Louis Stevenson	November 13
Dylan Thomas	October 27
Ted Turner	November 19
Kurt Vonnegut Jr.	November 11

MORE FAMOUS SAGITTARIANS

Woody Allen	December 1
Larry Bird	December 7
Kenneth Branagh	December 10
Arthur C. Clarke	December 16

Joe DiMaggio	November 25
Jimi Hendrix	November 27
Scott Joplin	November 24
C. S. Lewis	November 29
Margaret Mead	December 16
Bette Midler	December 1
Branch Rickey	December 20
Cathy Rigby	December 12
Rainer Maria Rilke	December 4
Monica Seles	December 2
Steven Spielberg	December 18
Grover Washington Jr.	December 12

MORE FAMOUS CAPRICORNS

Alvin Ailey	January 5
Muhammad Ali	January 17
Evangeline Booth	December 25
Louis Braille	January 4
Robert Duvall	January 5
George Foreman	January 10
Benjamin Franklin	January 17
Joe Frazier	January 17
Kahlil Gibran	January 6
Alexander Hamilton	January 11
Robert Joffrey	December 24
James Earl Jones	January 17
Janis Joplin	January 19
Johannes Kepler	January 6
Rudyard Kipling	December 30
Lucretia Mott	January 3
Sir Isaac Newton	January 4
Richard Nixon	January 9
Dolly Parton	January 19
Elvis Presley	January 8
Cokie Roberts	December 27

Diane Sawyer   December 22
Sissy Spacek   December 25

MORE FAMOUS AQUARIANS

Marian Anderson   February 17
John Belushi   January 24
Nicolaus Copernicus   February 19
Thomas Edison   February 11
Mia Farrow   February 9
Betty Friedan   February 4
Galileo   February 15
Alan Lloyd Hodgkin   February 5
Paul Newman   January 26
Ronald Reagan   February 6

MORE FAMOUS PISCES

Ralph Abernathy   March 11
Elizabeth Barrett Browning   March 6
Kurt Cobain   February 20
Ralph Ellison   March 1
Julius Erving   February 22
Theodor Geisel   March 2
George Harrison   February 24
Victor Hugo   February 26
Holly Hunter   March 20
Jackie Joyner-Kersee   March 3
Jack Kerouac   March 12
Camryn Manheim   March 9
Ralph Nader   February 27
Anaïs Nin   February 21
Elizabeth Taylor   February 27
George Washington   February 22